Floating Images

Eduardo
Souto de Moura's
Wall Atlas

Floating Images

EDUARDO SOUTO DE MOURA'S WALL ATLAS

Edited by
André Tavares and Pedro Bandeira

Lars Müller Publishers

9 **Everything Is Architecture**
Pedro Bandeira

33 **EDUARDO
SOUTO DE MOURA'S
WALL ATLAS**

125 **Souto de Moura's
"Cabinet de Curiosités"**
Philip Ursprung

135 **Amarcord: Analogy and Architecture**
Diogo Seixas Lopes

149 **A Rather Unscientific Autobiography**
Eduardo Souto de Moura

Everything Is Architecture

Pedro Bandeira

We begin with a contradiction; we write words in a book that should contain only images, a book meant to be an atlas in the overarching ambition of an infinite imagined collection. We thought of Aby Warburg's *Atlas Mnemosyne* and André Malraux's *Musée Imaginaire,* or Gerhard Richter's *Atlas,*[1] we thought of the *Albums* of Hans-Peter Feldmann, of the 3,000-odd photos from the *Visible World* of Peter Fischli and David Weiss,[2] or the *History of Architecture in All Countries from the Earliest Times to the Present Day* by James Fergusson, a history that reminds us of that brief nineteenth-century illusion where possession of all images corresponds to possession of all comprehension of the world.[3]

In Greek mythology, the colossal divine force signified by the word *atlas* is also associated with a savage nature linked to chaos and disorder, punished by Zeus with the task of supporting the burden of heaven and earth. Inherent to the totalitarian ambition of any such atlas is an entropy we might call inhuman because it results from an excess of information that can't be assimilated. The immeasurable amount of information available on the Internet is quite likely the best illustration of this utopia, or rather, dystopia, because the intrinsic gain from such environment

1 Gerhard Richter, *Atlas of the Photographs, Collages and Sketches,* New York, Distributed Art Publishers, 1997.

2 Peter Fischli, David Weiss, *Mundo visível,* Porto, Fundação de Serralves, 2001.

3 James Fergusson, *A History of Architecture in All Countries from the Earliest Times to the Present Day,* London, John Murray, 1874 (1st ed. 1865).

Gerhard Richter, *Atlas Sheet no. 7,* 1962
André Malraux selecting images for *Le Musée Imaginaire,* circa 1947

4 James Monaco, *The New Wave: Truffaut, Godard, Chabrol, Röhmer, Rivette,* Oxford University Press, 1976: "We could say that the limits of language are the limits of the world ... that the limits of my language are the limits of my world. And in that respect, I limit the world, I decide the boundaries. And when logical, mysterious death finally abolishes these limits ... and when there are, then, neither questions nor answers ... everything will be out of focus."

5 Jean-Luc Godard, *Deux ou trois choses que je sais d'elle,* France, 1967.

6 Antonio Esposito, Giovanni Leoni (eds.), *Eduardo Souto de Moura,* Milan, Electa, 2003. *El Croquis: Eduardo Souto de Moura 2005–2009,* no.146, Madrid, El Croquis Editorial, 2009.

punishes us with an awareness of impossibility—impossibility of absorption, control, limit, and content.

It is due especially to this excess of information and images that constantly assails us that we do not stop trying to build a filter, which henceforth reveals a personalized understanding of reality— even when "personalized" still means the result of the individual's acculturation before a society that is nowadays indifferently close by or foreign. What interests us is that the vastness of the world and the represented world make it impossible to build an atlas that is not legitimized by a condition or specific conditioner that mirrors a reality inevitably broken down into micronarratives. The question immediately arises as to whether we can continue calling Atlas a vision collected from a world shattered in the illusion of the individual, the individual's possible viewpoint.

But in the same way that "the limits of my language are the limits of my world. And in that respect, I limit the world, I decide the boundaries."[4]—it should therefore be possible to say that what I consciously or even inadvertently abdicate and ignore will also help define the world, with the supposed specificity of some "I," from another world, another atlas, emerging in the incommunicability or silence, so illusory "since ... since ... since I can't tear myself away from the objectivity that crushes me or the subjectivity that exiles me."[5]

In a television interview with Eduardo Souto de Moura, a diverse group of images could be seen in the background on his office

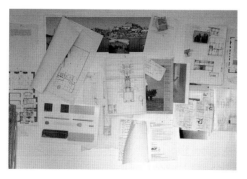

Atelier Eduardo Souto de Moura, 2010

walls: drawings of recent projects; a photo of the view from a La Tourette window; the water towers of Bernhard and Hilla Becher; an oil platform, perhaps in the North Sea; two women wearing burqas and snapping pictures on their cell phones; a section of the Tower of Pisa as if it had been designed to lean; the Murça sow statue, in which the roughly sculpted granite fades into the pattern on newsprint paper; a photo of Herberto Hélder, among other faces and other drawings.

On the wall, with no recognizable hierarchy, images deriving from the studio's own production (sketches and faxes about ongoing projects) mysteriously engage with images cut out from newspapers or magazines.

When we first approached Eduardo Souto de Moura, we were only sure about what we didn't want to do: a monograph. It would be hard and most likely redundant to compete with the 447-page volume by Electa,[6] with *El Croquis* issue no. 146, or the editions by Werner Blaser, Francesc Zamora Mola or (and) Aurora Cuito,[7] among so many other publications that have accompanied the career of one of the most widely publicized Portuguese architects and now winner of the Pritzker Prize. Yet those small generic cuttings on the office wall draw our attention due to the strangeness of the direct confrontation with images of architectural plans. When we proposed doing an atlas conditioned by a specific area, we knew it would have to contain those other-images on the rapidly proven hunch that, given knowledge's complexity, they could also be used for the architectural plan. In the end, as Hans Hollein defended more than forty years ago: "Everything is architecture,"[8] two burqas and two cell phones are architecture.

We know that architecture, as opposed to the so-called "exact" sciences, does not result from a merely deductive and "intelligent" process,[9] rationally demonstrating based on the sum of different parts. Rather the contrary, as Mark Wigley asserts: "There is no sane, reasonable, credible explanation for what happens in an architecture firm, but the firm is itself certainly a work of architectural intelligence."[10] Architecture as creative expression, along with other arts, will always be the result of complex, transdisciplinary, intuitive processes that imply in their authorial[11] and

7 Werner Blaser, *Eduardo Souto de Moura. Stein Element, element stone*, Basel, Birkhäuser, 2003. Francesc Zamora Mola (ed.), *Eduardo Souto de Moura, architect*, Barcelona, Loft, 2009. Aurora Cuito (coord.), *Eduardo Souto de Moura*, Lisbon, Dinalivro, 2004.

8 "Alles ist Architektur" in the original. What mainly interests us in this 1968 manifesto is the open desire that architecture should necessarily not be exhausted in the material existence of the building, that it should encompass expression based on "effects" and "emotional needs." See: "Everything Is Architecture," Joan Ockman (ed.), *Architecture Culture 1943–1968*, New York, Columbia Books of Architecture / Rizzoli, 1993, p. 462.

9 Eduardo Souto de Moura provokes: "Hell is full of *intelligent* projects but I add: to be a good architect you can't be very intelligent because that atrophies the practice of architecture – it needs a certain levity, it needs a certain lack of rigor. You can't have all the information. We have to take risks, become lame and then get a peg leg and walk better. Lots of knowledge leads to an Olympian vision that then doesn't work ..."

10 "Welcome to the Vacuum" (interview with M. Wigley by J. Moreno), *Jornal Arquitectos*, no. 239 May / June 2010, pp. 30–35.

11 It may seem untimely to insist on architecture as an authorial creation. We know it is becoming nowadays more and more a team practice, extremely conditioned by regulations and technical demands.

poetic expression the healthy confrontation of objectivity and subjectivity, science and art, rule and exception. And while architecture essentially persists as a "specialist in generalities," the mixing of images should come as no surprise—rescued from different origins and sharing the same place (the wall), to build something new and necessarily beautiful ... and false.

Various questions immediately arise: Do the images have an isolated value of their own or does that value derive from their association? Do they remain linked to their origin, do they keep a reference, or are they legitimately decontextualized? Do the images exist on this support due to their content or their superficial form? Are they sought with specific intent or casually found? Do they have an ephemeral meaning or do they express a desire to be forever? Are they a means, a vehicle, or an end? Do they comprise a whole, comprise an archive? Can they be appropriated? Are they worth more than a thousand words? Are they reality or representation? Do they simulate or replace the object? And above all: how do they relate to the planning and thinking of architecture?

As unbelievers in a contrasted black-and-white reality (images can be all and none of this), we imagine that background wall as a vestige of an ambiguous mental map between determinism and chance, denouncing the same distance we'll find in the space that wavers between the architectural plan and the work or between the built work and its later appropriation or perception. There will always be an observer who legitimizes the relativism, but under the title *Floating Images: Eduardo Souto de Moura's Wall Atlas,* we aim to stratify in an illusorily objective manner the images taken as methodology for thinking out the architecture project.

At a time when architecture seems to be giving way to new paradigms (in which the discipline seems to lose its autonomy, in which regulations seem meant for mindless architects, in which only specialization seems to legitimize architectural production, and in which low-cost competition results in a shortage of time and quality), these *Floating Images* assert themselves as a vestige of a time and method that will not stop representing a certain sense of resistance and will consequently also not stop justifying the exceptional nature of an architect and a work that can be copied only naively and superficially. This architecture, as Álvaro Siza says, needs time that's not there today. However, there is no nostalgia in this sense of loss. Eduardo Souto de Moura always knew how to stand against every expectation. He is, when least expected, unpredictable.

By focusing our attention on images on a wall in order to use them to legitimize a method, we are consciously withdrawing from another field of references linked to the word. This risk (which we hope will be lessened by the written contributions) is evident in the precept that "generally, the philosophers since Plato have always seen in the image an inferior form of representation, that is, an obstacle to thought. Traditional philosophy is dualist: image is on the side of the material, authentic thought is immaterial. To think, one has to go beyond images."[12] We can go even farther by stating that thought is "previous" to images, "previous" to the word itself. Even so, maybe what most appeals to us in the risk of focusing almost solely on images is precisely the abdication from "authentic thought" (which in Plato's *Republic* was attributed solely to God) in favor of thought that does not necessarily live from the antonym "authentic" but which lets itself be corrupted by subjectivity, superficiality, or even falseness. It is not by chance that we find cuttings on the wall of Eduardo Souto de Moura's office that read: "To make the truth more probable, we must necessarily add the false" (Fyodor Dostoyevsky); "What

12 Sylvain Auroux, Yvonne Weil, *Dicionário de Filosofia*, Porto, ASA, 1993, p. 205 (3rd ed.).

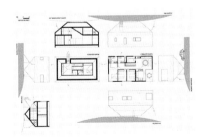 

Eduardo Souto de Moura, house on Douro II, Mesao Frio, 2004;
Hotel-Spa Aquapura, Alentejo, 2008

has been believed by everyone, always, everywhere, is in all likelihood false" (Paul Valéry); or "We have art in order not to die of truth" (Friedrich Nietzsche).

False can't be at the beginning and truth can't be at the end. In the words of Eduardo Souto de Moura: "There are two levels: one is the process of realization, in which the false ab initio is shocking. But after the process is consolidated I have to have the ambition to be a poet and do art because I believe that art has to be false ... if it is true ... well, the ethic is boring, so the aesthetic must be false! Artists have to work on the razor's edge, between true and false. What's false is not the support point for saying 'I'm going to lie'; falseness is the maximum point of autonomy, in which I'm dealing with things only for pure enjoyment, only so that Kant can reach the sublime. I know that with the truth I won't get there."[13]

As can be easily understood, to return to our initial contradiction, it is hard to get around the word even when we want to stress the contribution of image in the scope of an architectural project method. But this special attention to image is legitimized in our opinion in the major revolution of architectural project methodologies: the invention of drawing and perspective. While architectural knowledge and production were until that point essentially linked to the oral or written word transmitted in the professional guilds, the invention of rigorous drafting (plans, sections, elevations, perspective) gave the architectural plan an authorial aura,

Advertising photograph for Mercedes-Benz
with Le Corbusier's Weissenhofsiedlung in the background,1938

linking it to a sense of foresight, assuring an ideal of perfection, regardless of when the work was completed or even its materialization. The drawn representation, the image, became what was closest to the idea and the thought.

13 Souto de Moura, *op. cit.*, 2010.

The images that nowadays seek to communicate architecture tend to do so in an all-encompassing manner, decoded from the technical standpoint. Architecture as public art has the obligation to reach different publics. The most recent representation technologies have sharply increased the plausibility rates of images, leaving the observer to permanently question what is called reality. But this doubt, contrary to worry or anguish, seems to feed fascination about the fiction, not in its utopian or distant meaning, but something closer, something presented as possibility or alternative to a world increasingly more imprisoned in rules and regulations. And if somewhat paradoxically no (political, social, economic) stability whatsoever is assured, it will not be unusual to affirm that we are nowadays more prepared to live with uncertainty. Images and their inherent subjectivity will not stop being associated with the best of uncertainty, that is, desire and fear: that which we recognize even though, for us, it doesn't exist.

It is precisely in this space of the images' subjectivity, in what remains open, that appropriation is permitted, the personalization of its meaning. The images replicate what is also the architecture: a device that shelters or intermediates some action or expectation. In their condition as "means," the images along with the architecture should not be taken as an "end" in themselves.

Even so, perhaps the images lend themselves more to subjectivity than the buildings do. Images are light, they are surface (easily confused with superficiality), they are more permissive because they are more exposed to circulation and reproduction without the "aura" of the Benjamin stigma. They nowadays propagate as easily as a virus, ignoring borders (political, social, cultural), provoking seduction or rejection in observers and, necessarily, disdain. We live surrounded by images: the (past) century of images and their mass consumption; and the (future) century of images and their mass production. Images are thus democratized along with their production. As a result, the codes and their specificity in the scope of mass communication have fallen. There will surely be some residual resistance, but even pure scientific illegibility or artistic abstraction will at the very least find room in the universities, museums, or shopping centers. And if architects often use top-of-the-line automobiles in photomontages to enhance their projects' credibility, the auto industry also uses landmark buildings as backdrops for its advertising. Both images end up resembling each other. "Everything is architecture." Everything is image.

As everything is potentially circulating information, it becomes evident that not everything can be assimilated; there is a clear disproportion between what is made available and what is received. "Information" doesn't necessarily mean "communication," for information excess can even lead to incommunicability, a common entropy of our times, which refers to the human "incapacity" to process so much data. But we should recognize that the supposed "incapacity" derives from a complex system of filters that for our protection and pragmatism implies an extremely selective albeit not necessarily rational memory. In our brain we neither store nor stop storing information derived from a merely logical or deductive process. There is an intuition, occasionally irresponsible, that constantly leads us to ignore or choose images subconsciously—images that sink in and emerge unexpectedly to reveal a seeming absence of meaning—like the recollection of Rosebud in *Citizen Kane*.[14]

We aim to defend the view that this (deductive/intuitive) complexity is inherent not only to the specificity of each person's knowledge but also inherent to the specificity of the method and processes of conceiving and planning architecture. Beyond seeking the specific meaning of each of the images on Eduardo Souto de Moura's wall, we seek the inherent meaning of their selection and combination. We seek their legitimizing sense for the project without ignoring the risks we're taking, among them the risk of "simulacrum and simulation," in a direct reference to Jean Baudrillard. But as Souto de Moura asserts: "Perhaps the first state is simulation: things are lighter nowadays, they're not as thick—by living the image, we dispense with the object, we live its representation, we live in this kind of society … But it's not worth being a moralist; we have to know how to handle this, so that that 'evil' can have a different status and attain a status of poetry—some time ago, I wrote that 'poetry' is what remains …"[15]

We visited the walls of Souto de Moura's office in Aleixo, we visited the walls of his house in Porto's Foz district, we visited a discreet archive somewhere in the city. We opened drawers and notebooks. Images have an expiration date: a short time in the office, a middling time at home, and a long time in the archive; and in the same order they are intense, soft, and forgotten. Of course, it's not always that way. The house designed by Souto de Moura, with a low ceiling and enviable comfort, might also be deemed an archive given what's accumulated there: the walls filled with pictures and paintings; portraits and objects that compete with books for top spots on shelves; framed photos on the ground, leaning against the skirting board (does it exist?); images calmly waiting for a place on the wall; a time of affectation and representativeness. The archive is not exactly an archive in the strictest sense of the term. There is no concern for cataloguing. There is no concern about posterity: "My posterity is this one. I'm interested only in the present."[16] The models are kept in polystyrene boxes closed with brown tape, which gives them an informal, almost annoying aspect. Metal drawers hold postcards, Kodak slides, collaborators' portfolios, client proposals, sketchbooks—diverse things but which unexpectedly seem to construct

14 Orson Welles, *Citizen Kane,* United States, 1941.

15 Souto de Moura, *op. cit.,* 2010.

16 Ibid.

 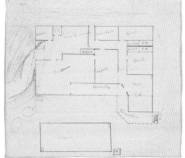

Atelier Eduardo Souto de Moura, archive, 2010
Eduardo Souto de Moura, draft for a house

a narrative. An archivist or historian here would try to work out a timeline, separating subjects, assigning categories. In our condition as architects, almost always more seduced by form than by content, we make no hierarchies. Everything is placed on a horizontal table plan that, unlike a "board," tends, in Georges Didi-Huberman's words, to stabilize content: it is the "crystallized beauty of the board, its found centripetal beauty, proudly steady, exhibited as a trophy" that stands against the working table as a "fractured beauty, a surface of transient encounters and gatherings, always allowing to correct or modify, or receive without hierarchy."[17] These *Floating Images,* as a vertical device, will still be a "table" although it now presents itself crystallized in book format.

The flattened pack of Camels with the pyramids of Egypt, a Romanian one-leu bill with a suspect palace, the almost pornographic eroticism of the Corinth Canal (or Braga Stadium), four bottles of wine floating in the cloudy sky of the Grão Vasco Museum; an inexpert plan, probably a house surveyed by a trainee or a project proposal ineptly drawn by a client; sketches made on vomit bags on one trip or another; a restaurant napkin and a project perspective ironically next to the phrase "Like it? Come back another time."

These *Floating Images,* the "table" crystallized in its book form, were accompanied by Eduardo Souto de Moura, who had abdicated the last word in the final selection of images (in their order

Grão Vasco Museum, Viseu, advertising for Dão wines
Un Leu bill, Romania

and association), expecting to be surprised by a new narrative built on images he knows so well. As is easily noticeable, this was not the only possible organization. It could have been from A to Z or from Z to A.[18] Maybe it would be more consistent to publish this atlas as loose-leaf pages like a game of cards, the way Charles and Ray Eames did, but then it would hardly be a book. Within the rigid structure of glued and sewn binding, an option was chosen, but there was no desire to explain it, so as to avoid the risk of conditioning stimulation about other reading possibilities. This subjective presentation of images certainly does not invalidate the attempt to objectively analyze their specific meaning in the process of conceiving architecture (in an overall manner) or in the project methodology (in the particular case).

We can (transversally) recognize four major groups framing these images: images that emerge in the area of project "conception" and to a certain degree precede it; images that emerge during project "production" and work with it; images that emerge in project "communication," almost always subsequent images; and finally images that emerge with the materialization of the work, its "reception," images that affirm their appropriation by others. In professional practice these groups interrelate to such an extent that this distinction doesn't always make sense, but to radically abstain from this layered reading would be like believing in the (unreachable but ever pursued) perennial utopia whereby the same image can depict the "conception," "production," "com-

17 Georges Didi-Huberman, *Atlas. Como llevar el mundo a cuestas?*, Madrid, Museo Nacional Centro de Arte Reina Sofía, 2010, p. 18.

18 Reference to the organization of subjects presented by Souto de Moura at the conference titled *What I Learned with Architecture*, from *Z to A?* in the context of the 80th anniversary of the publication *Casabella*. The conference was repeated at Porto Casa da Música and later at the School of Architecture of the University of Minho, Guimarães.

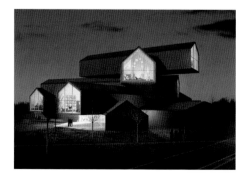

Herzog & de Meuron, VitraHaus, Weil am Rhein, 2006–09

munication," and "reception" phase of the architectural work, closing a perfect cycle. Contemporary architecture actually seems to be moving in this direction, for all arguments defending the new technologies used to represent and digitally and algorithmically conceive buildings seem based on closing the distance between the conception and materialization of buildings: more foresight and control; more control and relationship with production; greater accuracy of project images; and, no less important, more aesthetic and formal resemblance of the architectural object to its own digital image. Reality is apparently trying to imitate simulation, and in this regard we can say that form no longer follows function—form follows representation![19]

Bearing in mind that images in the context of the "production," "communication," and "reception" of Eduardo Souto de Moura's work have been widely disseminated in monograph form, in this first text we focus our attention on those that contribute to the broader field of his visual culture, in the belief that directly or indirectly, consciously or subconsciously,[20] some of these images concern (stimulate and condition) the thinking of architecture. It is in the relationship between a prior selection of diverse images and the aforementioned "conception" phase that we risk the following categories, which may eventually be useful in understanding the operative scope of these *Floating Images:*

Eduardo Souto de Moura, screen print of a drawing on a paper towel

Arbitrary Images

These are images found by chance. Not that chance may not result from something premeditated, from the habits of buying newspapers, magazines, or postcards. But the arbitrary images emerge occasionally; they are almost always images unexpected in their content, isolated images; they do not build a collection, nor a narrative beyond themselves. Yet they are still expectant images, for they are cut out and kept because of a feeling that they may one day be useful, as if illustrating a more lasting thought (two Japanese sumo wrestlers face off, to later depict the architect/client relationship—the first uses the second's rash move to knock him over). They are almost always beautiful on the surface and easily survive being taken out of their original context. Sometimes they're kept with no destination. They're tucked away in a drawer (a kneeling child reads a book to an attentive kneeling elephant and we'll never know why, though we can imagine).

Affective Images

These are images that are pursued. They are images with which we identify, almost as if we could have been the ones who made them. We are their fictional authors. They say what we'd like to have said. But they're better, they say better, and they said it first, and that's why we respect them, for what they fill out of our incapacity. They are images to take home, to eat and sleep with, and are shown there only shyly though they're always representative; we want them to be representative and at the same time are afraid that the somewhat public aspect might erase the personal affection we feel for them. We want and don't want to share them. The affection for these images almost always reverts to affection for their authors. These images must have a history; they have an associated memory but are unlikely to have a future because they can't be more than what they already are. They are images we believe to be stable—eternal (Ângelo de Sousa will surely know what we're talking about).

19 The photographs of the latest Vitra space designed by Herzog & de Meuron can hardly be distinguished from simulated images of the project phase. Buildings have never resembled their rendering images this closely.

20 "The architect works by manipulating memory, there's no doubt about this, consciously though most of the time subconsciously." Álvaro Siza, *Imaginar a Evidência*, Porto, Edições 70, 2000, p. 37.

Latent Images

These are images that exist transversally to everything that's done. They are technical images in the sense that they enable a direct relationship with the project. They are images of architecture, classic images (not necessarily of classical architecture) that are at the base of the architectural culture of almost everyone (Athens 1:36 color slides printed on Kodak film). They can arise at any moment; it's inevitable. They result from a visible legacy, from a relationship with a specific context; they are imposed from the outside. Their exceptional nature makes them ordinary because of their redundant appearance, their universality helps communicate ideas. Sometimes their uncomfortable omnipresence, their uncomfortable perfection, inhibits action. Love, hate. Sometimes they have to be contested, to find supposed contradictions in them (Mies van der Rohe in the Greek amphitheater of Epidaurus; a Barcelona Pavilion sketchbook with the cover of a donkey pulling a cart). We build ourselves with these images but it is in their distance that we gain the autonomy needed for the authorial creative sense. They are reminiscent images because no matter how much they try to overcome or forget, they will always exist as ghosts.

Analogical Images

These are images resulting from a provocative strategy—images that try to explain the unexplainable. They are images that help stimulate the project when it doesn't seem to find an intrinsic and disciplinary reason for its own program. In this regard they are images imported from other contexts that in a freely comparative relationship resolve or synthesize the project's essence. These analogical images can have a formal expression, approaching Rossi's methodology (the pillars of an oil platform in the North Sea transformed into a structure of the Trindade subway station); or a conceptual expression (the two women in burqas with cellphone cameras, alluding to the paradox between modesty that hides and technology that allows things to be seen—image for a

Middle Eastern project?). But there are also analogical images that arise after the project phase; such images can eventually help provide an other-explanation. They are the expression of coincidence, increasingly recurrent coincidences in a world increasingly full of images (compare the Quinta do Lago House with the sixteenth-century Nossa Senhora da Luz Church in Tavira—we know the house appeared before the image, even though the church appeared before the house).

21 Eduardo Souto de Moura was educated amidst collections. His father, an ophthalmologist, was a collector, among other things, of "stamps of men with glasses."

Recurrent Images

These images seemingly acquire strength in a larger group of similar images. They have no inherent value alone but a meaning derived from their synergetic association. They do not necessarily derive from "types" (in the formal sense) but almost always derive from "themes" in an abstract sense (a pile of wood next to a pile of granite or a pile of bread). Their recurrence ends up arousing a sometimes exhaustive and almost always informal sense of collection.[21] Recognition of the collection is almost always associated with a more lasting theme than with the specific time of a single project; they are themes that accompany Souto de Moura's work in a broader sense (the module, the repetition, the eternal game between rule and exception). But there are other kinds of recurring images that comprise collections structured formally in essentially geometric abstractions that almost make one forget

Eduardo Souto de Moura, aerial view of the General Humberto Delgado monument, 1979; house for three families, Quinta do Lago, Almansil, 1984–89

their figurative link. In this regard the elevation of the Microsoft System Center, a closed zoom of a Latin America slum, an aerial view of São Paulo, or a satellite image of Bam (Iran) are no more than a collection of patterns, textures, or repetitions that emphasize the sense of recurrence in the openly superficial reading of the image. They are not political images.

Utopian Images

These images overlap the sense of utility; they are the pure expression of architectural art. They are images not subject to any compromise; they result from no commission. They are always self-proposals and have no agenda. They are or try to be the closest expression of authorial thought, and of architectural thought in its broadest disciplinary autonomy, removed even from their "own acts" of professional practice. They are images not conceived to be consequent; rather, they try hard to escape the need to be consequent; they escape the sense of rule and productivity. They are economic in the sense that they are content to be only images, only thought. This group is made up of sketches, collages, or other objects (work objects whose decontextualization in the gallery pursues the sense of "ready-made"). Sketches on the language of architecture, about history's legacy, about mirrored and inverted representativeness, about irony and perversity *(fascism as a cover-up)*.

Eduardo Souto de Moura, sketchbooks

The proposed categorization cannot be separated from some concepts that Eduardo Souto de Moura has used based on different
readings. The question of analogy evidently derives from Aldo
Rossi and the sense that "no one begins from nothing."[22] But in
The Architecture of the City,[23] Rossi also legitimizes a view of function not responsible for form. It is the form symbolic in itself, in
its geometry, in its lasting abstraction and image able to be copied
and recontextualized that interests Souto de Moura.

Based on Rafael Moneo,[24] Eduardo Souto de Moura defends
that architecture begins by being arbitrary; there's always something unexplainable behind any project—a "flash" in current
informal parlance. But then: "The project becomes more cohe-
sive or stronger the more we find means to justify the initial arbitrariness, until it seems obvious. The project is the search for
reasons for chance. The concept's arbitrariness will have to be
validated throughout the process or course."[25] That course takes
its time. Souto de Moura is aware that architecture is nowadays
done with images (based on images, to be image), yet still and at
the same time laments the lack of processes legitimizing arbitrariness in most contemporary architectural production: "The course
has been transformed into something fleeting and frivolous."[26]

It is to counter this ephemeral time that Souto de Moura joined
up with Álvaro Siza to defend project time and, with Távora,
the historic time. For Souto de Moura, architecture still has a
perennial sense, the expectation of continuity beyond the specific
time we vaguely call "contemporaneity." To that end we can state
that there is no contemporaneity without history nor without
future expectation, otherwise everything is just contemporaneity.
Overall, this atlas of images reflects the time of the course and
processes associated with the architectural plan. And the plan,
any plan, shows the relationship between acquired wisdom and
openness to the foresight inherent to experimentation. The architect thereby presumes to be a mediator of images, between past
and future, reserving the possible contemporaneity for the project.
If all goes well, the rest will make history.

As can be seen in its form, *Floating Images* is not linked to this
comfortably categorized reading because it is structured at a

22 Souto de Moura,
op. cit., 2010.

23 Aldo Rossi,
L'architettura della città,
Padova, Marsilio, 1966.

24 Rafael Moneo,
*Sobre el concepto de
arbitrariedad en arquitectura,* Madrid, Real
Academia de Bellas Artes
de San Fernando, 2005.

25 Souto de Moura,
op. cit., 2010.

26 ESM, interview.

distance and *a posteriori*. In essence, this atlas is a complex device far removed from objectiveness: it is static in support but dynamic and spontaneous in content; it is stable and pragmatic as method but unpredictable in effects and results—just as the specific development of each project is likewise unpredictable. We do not mean to say that it's not possible, at some distance from the wall, to recognize beyond the method a set of themes that transversally appear here and there in the work of Eduardo Souto de Moura, such as, by way of example: a certain romanticism regarding ruin; postmodern irony; the vernacular presence almost always iconographically expressed; the assumed difficulty of drawing the place of the window in a wall that is always too big; the section as a material exhibitionism of modernist and machine culture; some austerity as research for timelessness and flexibility on use; or, obviously, the pragmatism associated with a so-called "minimalist" aesthetic, once provocative when postmodernism seemed solely conditioned to classicist formalism. Likewise, while these *Floating Images* are largely constituted by loose and ephemeral items, it cannot be hidden that they cohabit with other more lasting references—they probably don't have to go up on the wall only because they are already interiorized. In this regard the *Floating Images* are perhaps the visible materialization of what must still be consolidated and learned.

There are, of course, other possible readings based on these *Floating Images*. More or less subtly, we can infer references to Wittgenstein or Thomas Bernhard, Glenn Gould or Miles Davis, Donald Judd or Joseph Beuys, Aldo Rossi or Robert Venturi, among others. Eduardo Souto de Moura defends the analogy between various disciplines because he believes that: "Everything ends up the same: the problems are all alike, whether in architecture, dance, or music ..."[27] Interdisciplinary relationships are evident, though all seem to be heading in the same direction: the thinking of architecture as cultural production and product, in a broad, transdisciplinary, and artistic sense.

Beyond technique, functionality, or economy (characteristics easily associated with his "minimalist design"[28]), Eduardo Souto de Moura's works seem to seek a sense of culture that mediates between the individual and society, between past and present, erudite and common, and, no less important, between science and art. We believe that these *Floating Images* of Souto de Moura express that complexity and will help counter any simplistic reading whose unfortunate result is the apparent "Souto-de-Mourazation"[29] of Portuguese architecture.

Eduardo Souto de Moura must to a certain degree be inadvertently responsible for this extended "counterfeiting" phenomenon. With the humbleness that characterizes great architects, Souto de Moura has always publicly expressed the importance of the "copy" in his training and career (in the teaching tradition inherited from the Beaux-Arts). But while the good student knows how to make his own what pertained to others, the bad student will be condemned to the "shame of someone who steals and then can't carry the load," to quote an old saying.

As an eventual "victim" of counterfeiting (at the same time synonymous with recognition and renown), Eduardo Souto de Moura's architecture is quickly circulated and publicized, and itself becomes an image in the atlases of other architects, thereby closing a cycle in the vast field of architectural culture. The way Souto de Moura's architecture finds "reception" is not absent from these *Floating Images:* when it's finished, the work is appropriated and often registered, revealing interpretations that surprise the architect himself. This is inevitable because architecture can only be an "end" in itself for architects; for everyone else

27 "The other day I was reading Igor Stravinsky's *Poetics of Music,* which seemed like an architecture book …"

28 This is surely the expression most often used to describe Eduardo Souto de Moura's architecture outside the more academic scope yet it is not necessarily an expression with which he would identify himself.

29 Nuno Grande, "Teatros del Mundo," *El Croquis: Eduardo Souto de Moura 2005–2009,* no.146, Madrid, El Croquis Editorial, 2009, p. 25.

Eduardo Souto de Moura, residential building in Praça de Liége, Porto, 1994–2001; house in Valongo, 2003–07

it will always be a "means" subject to eventuality. Luís Ferreira Alves—architecture photographer and friend of Eduardo Souto de Moura—recently visited the house of one of Souto de Moura's clients so that he could photograph it. The client was already living there, but before the visit he moved almost all his belongings outside into the garden. This was not for reasons of modesty or privacy, but because he thought the empty house would be more photogenic and more to the liking of the architect and photographer. Maybe he was successful, but Souto de Moura's somewhat ironic smile when he told us the story hinted that he would have preferred to photograph the surreal outside pile of furniture instead of the empty house. These *Floating Images* are basically about that discreet desire for complexity and contradiction.

Eduardo Souto de Moura, drawing of the Porto subway on an airsickness bag

Eduardo Souto de Moura, drawings of the Porto subway on airsickness bags

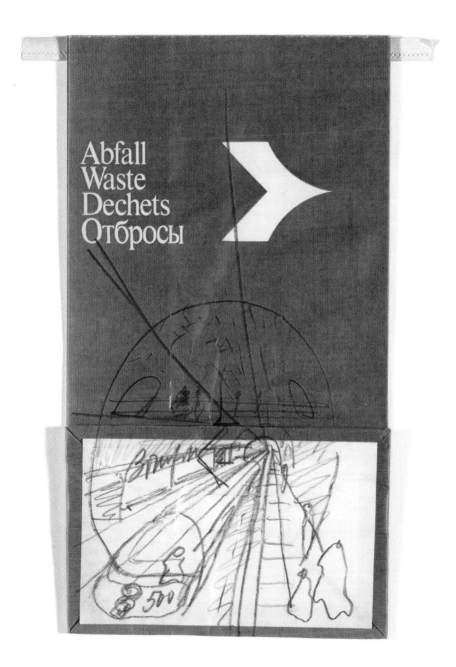

Abfall
Waste
Dechets
Отбросы

EDUARDO SOUTO DE MOURA'S WALL ATLAS

John Singer Sargent, *Atlas and the Hesperides*, 1922–25

Epidaurus, Greece, postcards

Mies van der Rohe in Epidaurus, Greece
Epidaurus, Greece
Eduardo Souto de Moura, Braga Municipal Stadium, 2000–04

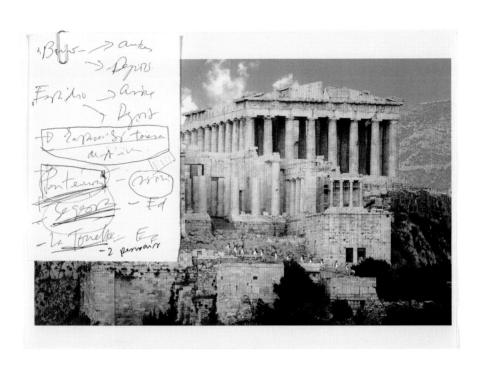

Notes attached to Parthenon image

Hermes, *Athens 1*, color slide collection on Kodak film

ACROPOLIS

ACROPOLIS

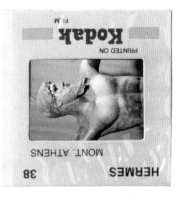

ATHENS

ACROPOLIS

ATHENS

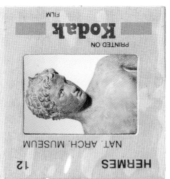

ATTICA — HERMES 31 ACROPOLIS MUSEUM — PRINTED ON Kodak FILM

HERMES 1 ACROPOLIS — PRINTED ON Kodak FILM

HERMES 2 — PRINTED ON Kodak FILM

HERMES 65 ATHENS — PRINTED ON Kodak FILM

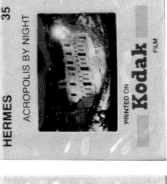

HERMES 35 ACROPOLIS BY NIGHT — PRINTED ON Kodak FILM

ATHENS — HERMES 2 — PRINTED ON Kodak FILM

HERMES 29 ATHENS BY NIGHT — PRINTED ON Kodak FILM

HERMES 2 ACROPOLIS — PRINTED ON Kodak FILM

Unidentified images

Newspaper clip

Armando Salas Portugal, Luis Barragan's gardens in El Pedregal, Mexico City
Unidentified images

Bunker images

Alessandra Chemollo and Fluvio Orsenigo, Punta Perotti, Bari

Alessandra Chemollo and Fluvio Orsenigo, *Buon Anno*,
envelope for photograph

Eduardo Souto de Moura, ruin restoration in Gerês, Vieira do Minho, 1980
Álvaro Siza, SAAL housing program, São Vítor, Porto, 1974–77

Unidentified image

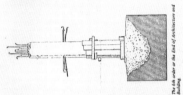

The 6th order or the End of Architecture and Building.

Eduardo Souto de Moura, *Internship Report*,
Escola Superior de Belas Artes do Porto, 1980
Le Corbusier in the Parthenon, 1911

Eduardo Souto de Moura, Braga Music School, 2009

Postcard
Ângelo de Sousa, Eduardo Souto de Moura,
out here: disquieted architecture, Portuguese representation,
La Biennale di Venezia, 2008

Postcard

Heinrich Tessenow, Stadtbad Berlin-Mitte, Berlin, 1927–30
Hans Döllgast, reconstruction of Leo von Klenze's partially destroyed Alte Pinakothek, Munich, 1952–57
Giorgio Grassi, Casa dello studente, Chieti, 1976–79
Heinrich Tessenow, Hellerau
Rafael Moneo, Ayuntamiento de Logroño, 1973–80
Álvaro Siza, Escola Superior de Educação, Setúbal, 1986–94

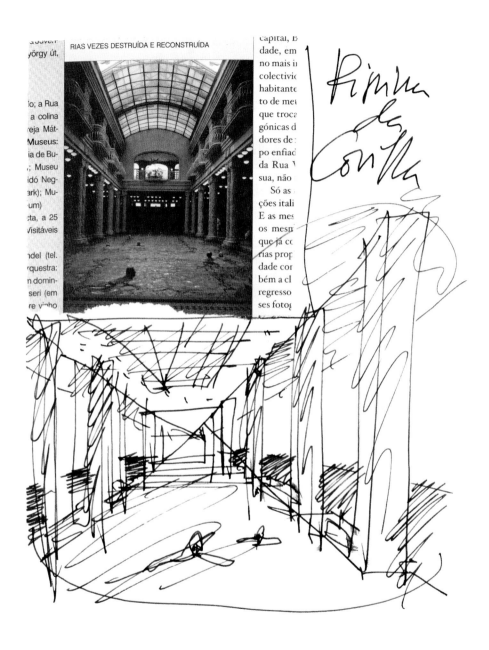

Eduardo Souto de Moura, drawing on newspaper clip, Gellért baths, Budapest

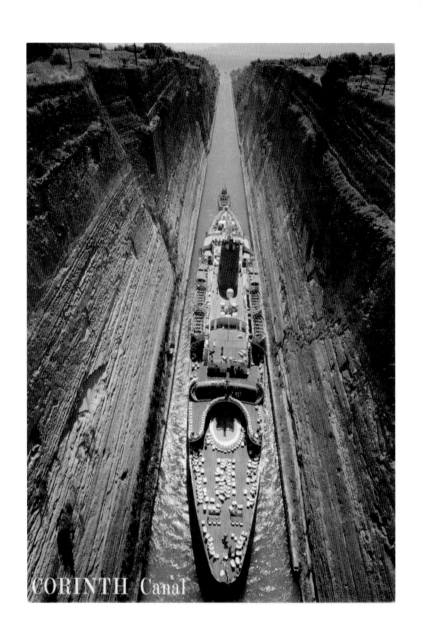

CORINTH Canal

Corinth Canal, postcards

KORINTHOS Canal

Garden of Fernando Távora's house, Quinta da Covilhã, in Guimarães

Oscar Niemeyer, Hotel, Brasília, 1958

Donald Judd, *Untitled Work in Concrete*, Marfa, 1980–84

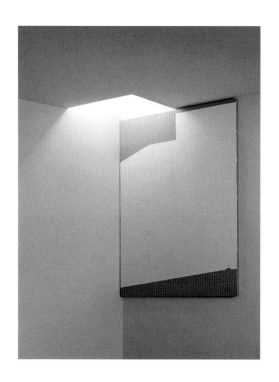

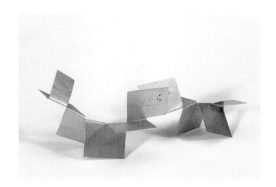

Installation of a Pedro Cabrita Reis painting
Ângelo de Sousa, study for a sculpture

Simon Ungers, *Erat Ecclesia* (*Once Were Cathedrals*), Leipzig, rendering, 2004
Amilcar de Castro, *Gigante Dobrada*
Eduardo Souto de Moura, extension to Kunstmuseum Basel, rendering, 2009

Ângelo de Sousa, untitled work, 1965

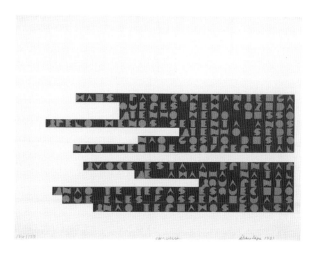

Álvaro Lapa, untitled work, 1993; *Conversa*, screen print, 1981

Eduardo Souto de Moura's library, Mies van der Rohe section

Escrito na pedra

Pensa-se a partir
do que se escreve
e não o contrário
Louis Aragon, escritor
francês (1897-1982)

Escrito na pedra

Compreendemos
a natureza resistindo-lhe.
Gaston Bachelard,
filósofo francês
(1884-1962)

Escrito na pedra

A arquitectura é música
petrificada.
Johann Goethe,
escritor alemão
(1749-1832)

Escrito na pedra

Temos a arte para não
morrer da verdade.
Friedrich Nietzsche,

Escrito na pedra

"Quando não temos
certezas, estamos vivos"
Graham Greene,
escritor inglês
(1904-1991)

Escrito na pedra

Nós somos o que fazemos.
O que não se faz não existe.
Portanto, só existimos nos
dias em que fazemos.
Padre António Vieira,
orador e escritor
português (1608-1697)

Escrito na pedra

São precisos 60 anos
e não 9 meses para
fazer um homem.
André Malraux, escritor
francês (1901-1976)

Escrito na pedra

"Os que vivem
intensamente não têm
medo de morrer."
Anaïs Nin, escritora
francesa (1903-1977)

Escrito na pedra

Cansei-me de ser
moderno. Quero ser
eterno.
Pablo Picasso, pintor
espanhol (1881-1973)

Escrito na pedra

Eu nunca penso
no futuro. Ele não
tarda a chegar.
Albert Einstein, físico
alemão (1879-1955)

Escrito na pedra

A arquitectura é a
vontade de uma época
traduzida num espaço.
Ludwig Mies van der
Rohe, arquitecto alemão
(1886-1969)

Escrito na pedra

Cinema-verdade?
Prefiro o cinema-mentira.
A mentira é sempre
mais interessante
do que a verdade.
Federico Fellini, cineasta
italiano (1920-1993)

...stupidificação em
Curso."
João Miguel Tavares
Correio da Manhã

Escrito na pedra

Publicamos para não
passar a vida a corrigir
rascunhos.
Jorge Luis Borges,
escritor argentino (1899-
1986)

Escrito na pedra

Esperar é um modo
de chegares
Um modo de te amar
dentro do tempo
Daniel Faria, poeta
português (1971-1999)

Escrito na pedra

Temos a arte para não
morrer da verdade
Friedrich Wilhelm
Nietzsche, filósofo
alemão (1844-1900)

d   *P. Mexia*

A beleza é passageira,
instável, letal, sempre
cobiçada e ameaçada. É
uma luta, uma obsessão,
uma angústia. A beleza
é uma forma de loucura

Escrito na pedra

Garantir que exista uma
arquitectura significativa
não é parodiar a história
mas articulá-la.
Daniel Libeskind,
arquitecto de origem
polaca (1946-)

Jornal Público, clips from the daily section "Escrito na pedra" (Written in Stone)

Escrito na pedra

Os homens jovens querem ser crentes e não são, os velhos querem ser descrentes e não podem.
Oscar Wilde, escritor irlandês (1854-1900)

Escrito na pedra

Para tornar a verdade mais verosímil, precisamos necessariamente de lhe adicionar a mentira.
Fiódor Dostoiévski, escritor russo 1821-1881)

Escrito na pedra

Agir, eis a inteligência verdadeira. Serei o que quiser. Mas tenho que querer o que for.
Fernando Pessoa, poeta português (1888-1935)

Escrito na pedra

Nada parece verdadeiro que não possa parecer falso
Michel Eyquem de Montaïgne, ensaísta e escritor francês (1533-1592)

Escrito na pedra

Ele não sabia que era impossível. Foi lá e fez.
Jean Cocteau, autor e realizador francês (1889-1963)

Governo de Salvação Nacional que deveria incluir o PCP."
Pedro Santana Lopes
Sol

Escrito na pedra

Não rezo porque não quero chatear Deus.
Orson Welles, realizador norte-americano (1915-1985)

Escrito na pedra

Não vás para onde o caminho te possa levar; vai antes por onde não há caminho e deixa rasto.
Ralph Waldo Emerson, filosófo norte-americano (1803-1882)

Escrito na pedra

Tem ideia de quanto mal nós fazemos por essa maldita necessidade de falar?
Luigi Pirandello, dramaturgo italiano (1867-1936)

Público de 30/11/09

Escrito na pedra

O que tem sido acreditado por todos, e sempre, e em toda a parte, tem toda a probabilidade de ser falso.
Paul Valéry, escritor francês (1871-1945)

Diário Económico

Escrito na pedra

"O cinema é a mais bela fraude do mundo"
Jean-Luc Godard (1930-), cineasta francês

Correio da Manhã

"A democracia precisa de um estado novo."
Manuel Serrão
Jornal de Notícias

Escrito na pedra

A viagem da descoberta consiste não em achar novas paisagens, mas em ver com novos olhos.
Marcel Proust, escritor francês (1871-1922)

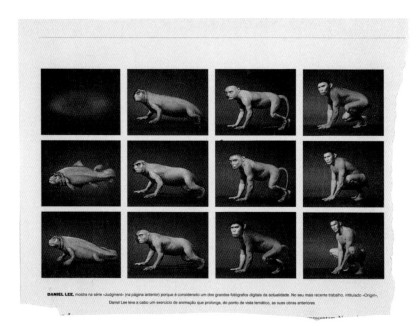

DANIEL LEE, mostra na série «Judgment» (na página anterior) porque é considerado um dos grandes fotógrafos digitais da actualidade. No seu mais recente trabalho, intitulado «Origin», Daniel Lee leva a cabo um exercício de animação que prolonga, do ponto de vista temático, as suas obras anteriores

Newspaper clip

Jornal Público, clips

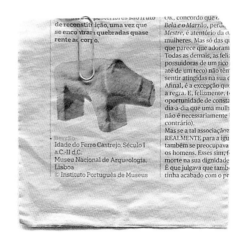

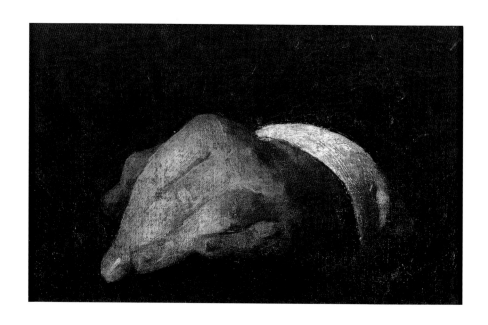

Silva Porto's hand painted by Columbano, 1875

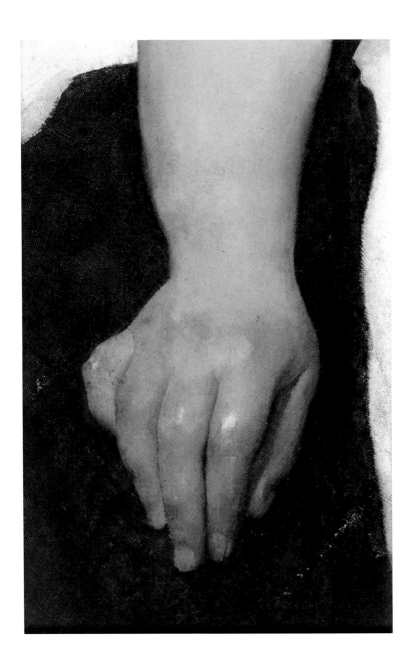

Woman's hand painted by Silva Porto

Nome científico: *Myrmecophaga tridactyla*. Ordem: *Xenarthra*. Família: *Myrmecophagidae*

JARDIM
ZOOLÓGICO

Newspaper clip

Jornal Expresso, clip, 2005

Newspaper clips

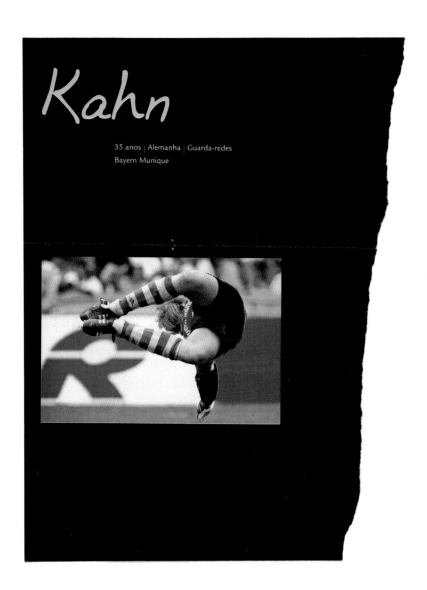

Kahn

35 anos | Alemanha | Guarda-redes
Bayern Munique

Newspaper clip

Newspaper clip

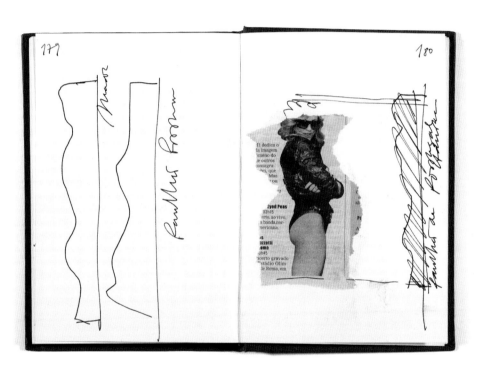

Eduardo Souto de Moura, sketchbook

Jornal Público, clip

Ver as ondas no deserto

É o cenário mais fotografado da América do Norte. Um jornalista céptico foi perceber porquê. Texto de Hugo Martin Fotografia de Spencer Weiner

Cigarette packs

ameaças e os ataques contra a sua integridade têm sido uma constante, a ponto de a maioria querer desistir.

cidade pelo *The Independent*. Sem os votos das mulheres, claro que esta eleição não será válida".

soida
critic
quéri

OMAR SBHANI/AFP

Paq
Talibaı
sub

● Un
ban p
mido
vimeı
terior
Mehsı
doenta
que co
por uı
realiza
secreto
acredi
ata

Mulheres de *burka* tiram fotografias com telemóvel num comício

Jornal *Público*, clip
Albano Silva Pereira, untitled photograph, 1991

Bisalhães black pottery

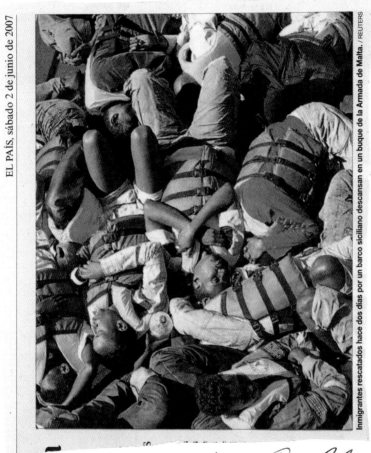

EL PAÍS, sábado 2 de junio de 2007

Inmigrantes rescatados hace dos días por un barco siciliano descansan en un buque de la Armada de Malta. / REUTERS

El País, Saturday, June 2, 2007

Luísa Penha, untitled work, roller-ball pen on paper, 2011

Newspaper clip, São Paulo
Unidentified images

Newspaper clip

Ajudar os sobreviventes
é a tarefa mais urgente em Bam

FIM DAS BUSCAS

Reconstrução da
cidade iraniana
devastada pelo
sismo começa a ser
equacionada

SOFIA RODRIGUES

As equipas humanitárias que
estão a trabalhar na cidade de
Bam voltaram a sua atenção
para a construção de abrigos
permanentes para acolher
milhares de iranianos desalojados na sequência do sismo
da semana passada.

As operações de busca e de
salvamento terminaram e,
na próxima semana, a ONU
irá apelar à angariação de
fundos para responder às necessidades básicas de abrigo,
alimentação e água, afirmou
à Reuters o coordenador das
Nações Unidas no local, Frederick Lyons.

Com a ajuda internacional
a chegar à área afectada, os estrangeiros consideram que se
diluíram os receios de riscos
para a saúde. "Não há registo
de doenças contagiosas", disse
Lyons.

A ajuda internacional continua a chegar ao aeroporto
de Bam. "Este é o oitavo ou
nono voo que trazemos e vão
continuar a chegar", disse um
membro da tripulação de um
Hércules C-130 paquistanês,
carregado de tendas e candeeiros de querosene.

No terreno, as autoridades locais e as organizações
humanitárias continuam a
trabalhar para cuidar dos
sobreviventes. O Crescente
Vermelho iraniano (equivalente à Cruz Vermelha) começou a instalar um hospital
com 250 camas, que deverá
gerir as unidades de saúde de
campanha abertas por equipas
estrangeiras.

Nas ruas de Bam, entre
as tendas que se amontoam
junto às casas em ruínas, funcionários iranianos fazem o
recenseamento dos desalojados para conhecer as suas
necessidades.

Os habitantes da cidade, que
actualmente não ultrapassam
os 40 mil, deverão ser reagrupados em campos de tendas
para facilitar a distribuição de
ajuda e o controlo sanitário.

A reconstrução de Bam começa agora a ser equacionada
por arquitectos e engenheiros.
A tarefa é enorme mas não é
impossível, disse à BBC o
responsável pela equipa de
reconstrução, Hamid Eskander, tendo em conta que só 30
por cento dos edifícios podem
ser restaurados. "As pessoas
não esquecem as suas casas,
vão voltar a reconstrui-las",
afirma o mesmo responsável,
acrescentando que foi constituído um tribunal especial
para investigar a eventual
construção ilegal na cidade.

Opinião bem mais pessimis-

ta é a de um arquitecto afogado
da associação Arquitectos de
Urgência, enviado numa missão ao local do sismo. "Não há
nada para recuperar em Bam",
afirmou à AFP Ashmat Froz,
que reside em França. "Nunca
vi nada assim. A vila foi inteiramente destruída. Não há
nada a recuperar para lá de
alguns materiais, como adobos, que podem ser utilizados
na reconstrução".

Para Hamid Eskander, o
padrão pobre de construção
das casas naquela região é,
em grande medida, o culpado pelo elevado número de

mortos. Por isso, adianta, a
reconstrução deverá usar as
mais recentes concepções
anti-sísmicas.

Aos poucos, a vida em Bam
começa a voltar à normalidade. Na próxima semana, as
aulas vão ser retomadas nas
cinco escolas da cidade, menos
danificadas pelo sismo.

**Indonésia e México
abalados por um sismo**

Uma pessoa morreu e 12 ficaram feridas na sequência de
um tremor de terra que abalou
ontem as ilhas indonésias de
Bali e Lombok. O sismo, que

registou uma magnitude de 6,1
na escala de Richter, causou
alguns estragos nas casas das
ilhas turísticas e provocou um
ataque cardíaco a um homem
que viria a ser a única vítima
mortal provocada pelo abalo.

Na ilha de Bali, o hospital
transferiu os doentes para
tendas no exterior, depois de
terem aparecido fendas nas
paredes. Sete templos hindus e
três mesquitas também sofreram alguns danos. O epicentro
do sismo situou-se entre as
ilhas de Bali e de Lombok, o
destino escolhido por muitos
turistas nesta época do ano

para passar o "reveillon".

Outro forte abalo atingiu
a costa do México, perto de
Acapulco, na quinta-feira,
mas não houve registo de
mortos ou de danos materiais
graves. O sismo, que registou
uma magnitude de 6,3 na escala de Richter, teve o epicentro
ao largo da vila piscatória de
Zihuatanejo, a 160 quilómetros
de Acapulco e a 400 da Cidade
do México. Duas réplicas mais
pequenas foram sentidas meia
hora depois e uma hora após
o primeiro abalo na capital do
México, apesar da distância a
que se situou o epicentro.

Imagens de Bam, captadas via satélite, antes e depois do sismo, mostram uma cidade quase destruída e irrecuperável

BUSH PEDE AOS AMERICANOS QUE COMAM CARNE DE VACA

Países mantêm embargo
às exportações
de produtos bovinos
dos Estados Unidos

O Presidente dos Estados Unidos, George W. Bush, pediu aos
norte-americanos que sigam o
seu exemplo e continuem a comer carne de bovino, apesar de
o primeiro caso da doença das
vacas loucas ter sido detectado
no país.

"Ainda hoje comi carne de
vaca e continuarei a fazê-lo",
assegurou o Presidente no
primeiro dia do ano.

Questionado sobre a necessidade de dar mais garantias aos
consumidores sobre a carne e
derivados de bovino, Bush disse ter dado instruções "a.fera
que sejam tomadas as medidas
necessárias para assegurar que
o aprovisionamento alimentar
é seguro" e garantia que o "norte-americano pode ter confiança [na carne que consome]".

Neste momento, os investigadores estão em vias de
confirmar se o animal contaminado com a doença em
Washington foi infectado no
Canadá, o seu local de origem.
Querem também perceber se o
caso de BSE detectado no ano
passado no Canadá e o norte-americano tiveram uma origem comum, já que ambos os
animais nasceram em Alberta
e poderão ter sido infectados
com o mesmo produto alimentar contaminado.

Mais de 30 países decretaram um embargo à carne de
vaca norte-americana desde
o passado dia 23 de Dezembro,
altura em que as autoridades dos EUA anunciavam o
primeiro caso de BSE. Além
das acções para manter a
confiança dos consumidores
norte-americanos, o Governo
está a lançar uma mega-operação para conseguir restaurar
a confiança internacional nos
seus produtos bovinos.

Equipas de peritos da administração Bush estiveram
em Tóquio e Seul no início da
semana e na terça-feira uma
outra delegação deslocou-se
ao México para discutir as
medidas de segurança adoptadas pelos produtores e pelas
autoridades dos EUA. Neste
momento, 44 mil toneladas
de carne de vaca americana,
avaliadas em 350 milhões de
dólares, que estavam em trânsito para os países importadores quando estes decretaram
o embargo, estão no alto mar
sem autorização para poderem
entrar nos países de destino.

Mas as tentativas de escoar
os produtos continuam. A
China tornava ontem pública
a apreensão de 168 toneladas de
produtos bovinos norte-americanos, que se destinavam a ser
vendidos, apesar do embargo
decretado pelo país.

Segundo o diário "Beijing
Qingnian Bao", esta é a segunda apreensão feita na China
depois de o país ter decidido
suspender as importações de
carne de vaca e derivados dos
EUA e aplicado uma série de
medidas de prevenção. ■

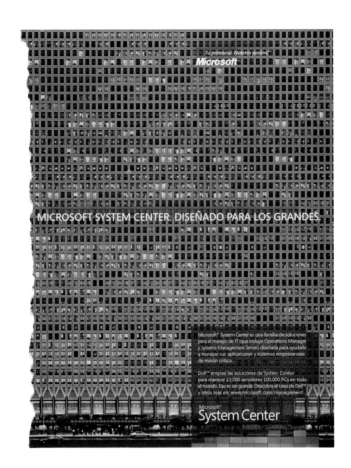

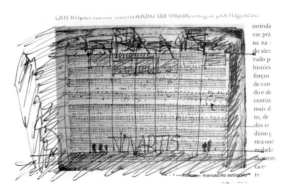

Microsoft System Center advertisement
Eduardo Souto de Moura, drawing on newspaper clip, 2006

querido Eduardo; te envío otra foto
de estratos para tu colección.
No es fácil...

un abrazo.

Genina, 94, Abril '15

Fax, Genina, April 1995

Wood pile, Unhão
Eduardo Souto de Moura, *Ordem Arq. VII*, 2010

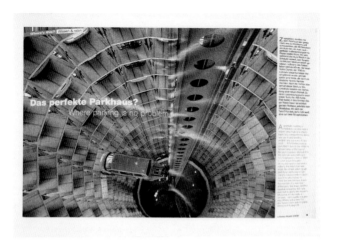

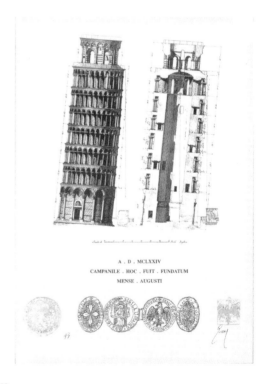

Lufthansa Magazin, February 2003
Pisa Tower, poster

Jornal Público, Friday, September 5, 2004
Eduardo Souto de Moura, postcard of a collage, May 3, 1991
Jornal Público, clip

Hans Hollein, Aircraft Carrier City in Landscape Project, 1964
Unidentified image

Eduardo Souto de Moura, *Project for the Middle East*, 2010
Unidentified images

Bernhard and Hilla Becher, *Coal Bunkers*, 1974

Eduardo Souto de Moura and Graça Correia, Fundação Robinson Auditorium, Portalegre, 2007

Gabriele Basilico, Matosinhos, 1995

Beatriz Luz, untitled work, 1992
Mario Sironi, *Paesaggio urbano*, 1927

Luísa Penha, drawing on plywood

A HOUSE BUILT BY FRANK LLOYD
WRIGHT FOR HIS SON – Basquiat

LARRAIN HOUSE
Cecilia Puga

HOUSING COOPERATIVE
Aldo Rossi

CARPENTER'S, MASON'S...PLACE
John Hejduk

CASA VAN MIDDELEM-DUPONT
Alvaro Siza Vieira

Eduardo Souto de Moura, image selection for Mobles 114 calendar, Barcelona, 2008

RUDIN HOUSE
Herzog & de Meuron

SPLITTING
Gordon Matta-Clark

CASA NOS AÇORES
Eduardo Souto de Moura

MOTHER'S HOUSE
Robert Venturi

CASA JOÃO, ANTES
J. Paulo dos Santos

ANÓNIMO - SEC. XX

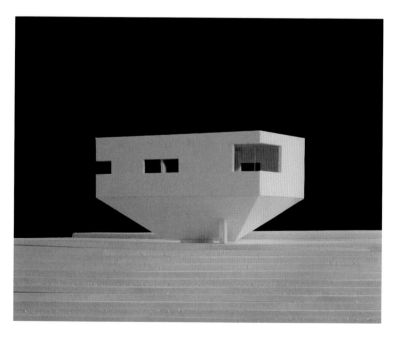

Tina Z'Rotz & Markus Schwander, 44°, Geschinen, Switzerland, 2008
Eduardo Souto de Moura, house in Douro II, Mesão Frio, 2004

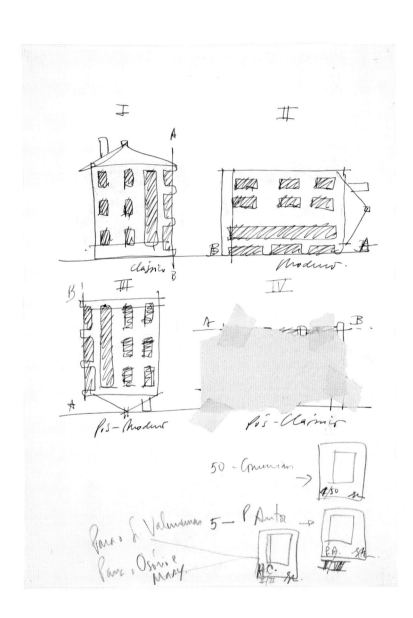

Eduardo Souto de Moura, sketch for screen print

Jackson Hole, Wyoming, panoramic view used in Mies van der Rohe's Resor House collage, 1937–41
Adalberto Libera, Casa Malaparte, Capri, 1937

Thomas Bernhard
Unidentified image
Le Corbusier, La Tourette, Éveux-sur-l'Arbresle, 1953-60, photograph and postcard

Mies van der Rohe in New York
Eduardo Souto de Moura's sketchbook
Mies van de Rohe, Farnsworth House, Illinois, 1945–51

This bedroom in one of the Pavilion Apartments commands a fine view of Passaic River and countryside beyond. On clear days the panorama is visible for 24 miles. To the east is Manhattan; to the west, wooded hills; to the south, the hub of downtown Newark.

Mies van der Rohe, Colonnade Park, Newark, newspaper clips, 1958–60
Eduardo Souto de Moura, Mies van der Rohe's Barcelona Pavilion sketch

10

los angeles:
between
dream and
reality
zwischen traum und wirklichkeit

Newspaper clip

Eduardo Souto de Moura, Burgo Tower, Porto, 1991–2007

Eduardo Souto de Moura, Braga Municipal Stadium, 2000–04, postcard and photograph

Eduardo Souto de Moura, Braga Municipal Stadium, 2000–04

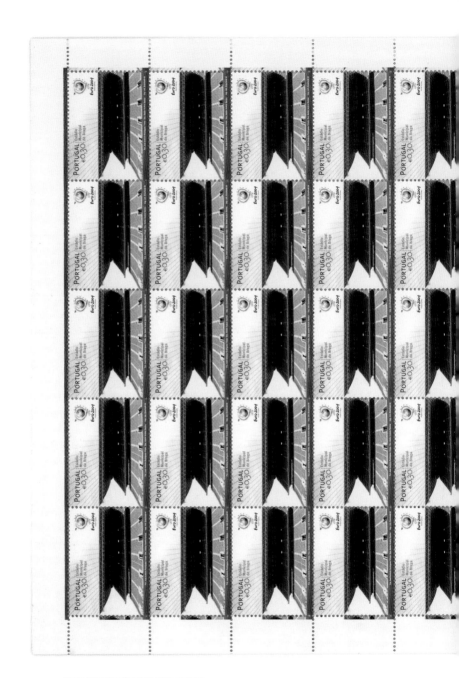

Braga Municipal Stadium, 2004, stamps

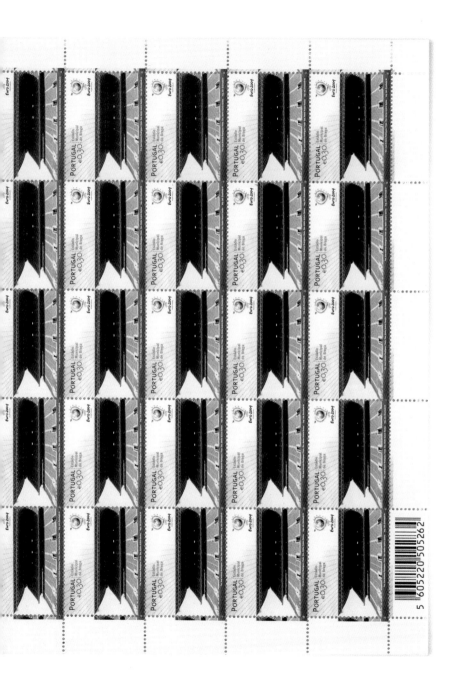

Church of Nossa Senhora da Luz, Tavira

Eduardo Souto de Moura, house for three families, Quinta do Lago, Almansil, 1984–89

Unidentified image

Unidentified image

Atelier Eduardo Souto de Moura, 2012

Souto de Moura's "Cabinet de Curiosités"

Philip Ursprung

As if Eduardo Souto de Moura partially resides in the realm of art, the atmosphere of his office recalls an artist's studio. Unlike many of his colleagues whose offices have adopted a business-style look with a lot of chrome, computer screens, and "clear desks"—perhaps to make corporate clients and representatives of communal authorities feel at home—Souto de Moura prefers to design with tangible, haptic media such as drawings and cardboard models and maintains a creative disorder in the place he works. Like Álvaro Siza, his mentor, colleague, friend, and neighbor, who works a floor above him, in the same building in Porto, he is more a "patron" than a manager. His office looks like an extension of a one-man studio, a microcosmos, a laboratory overflowing with plans and cardboard models, books, souvenirs, and other marvels. Souto de Moura's workplace is more a "cabinet de curiosités" than a "paperless studio."

The most striking features in the office of Eduardo Souto de Moura are the many images. Postcards, newspaper clippings, torn-out advertisements, family photos, depictions of his most

Atelier Eduardo Souto de Moura, 2010

recent buildings, photocopies and faxes, reproductions of works of art, drawings, floor plans, exhibition cards, an envelope of a cigarette pack, views of cities, etc., are randomly distributed on the office walls. Some images are simply pinned to the boards that surround the office. Others stand neatly framed on bookshelves, next to models, boxes full of photographs, books, magazines, and a seemingly endless collection of CDs and memorabilia of Miles Davis, Souto de Moura's hero. In some cases, the yellowish paper and the wrinkles show that the images must have been hanging there for several years, whilst others are torn out of yesterday's newspaper. In the meeting room, there is a group of clippings with quotes by famous writers, which Souto de Moura uses, he explains, when he is searching for a quote to use in a text or conference. The arrangement of the images changes regularly and, so it seems, extends from the office to the private home, where more images spread out. Once taken from the walls, the images are not discarded but collected in drawers and boxes, from whence they can reemerge and return to the walls. There is no inventory, no apparent order in the collection. Some items might get lost and disappear. Others might find their way into the notebooks, which Souto de Moura has kept since the beginning of his practice and which, unlike the images, he carefully organizes and keeps at hand as his personal archive.

Visual Theory

What are the relations between the images on the wall and ongoing projects of the studio? Of course, there are, as in every architectural office, some documentary photographs of built projects— such as the Braga Stadium or the Paula Rego Museum—which can be presented to visitors and clients. And there are many obvious analogies between images in the collection and completed projects. Some relate to the Braga Stadium—Eduardo Souto de Moura's most spectacular work to date—for instance, the postcards of the Antique theater of Epidaurus, which merges with the Arcadian landscape and the built structure. The same goes for the Corinth Canal, the very emblem of a very large sculpture cut into an existing terrain, so to speak. Another image depicts the concrete sculptures that Donald Judd placed in the landscape of Marfa, Texas, in the 1980s. The connection between the Minimalist arrangement and the way Souto de Moura has placed the horizontal building of the Burgo Tower in Porto on the ground is obvious. Another image stems from Paul Virilio's book *Bunker archéologie*.[1] It was taken by Virilio in the 1960s or early 1970s and shows a German concrete bunker from World War II half sunken in the dunes of France. It clearly resembles the tilted house in Ponte de Lima, probably Souto de Moura's most iconic building, and it is an emblem of the fact that every building is subject to the laws of nature and has a limited life span.

However, in most cases the relation between the images and the oeuvre of Eduardo Souto de Moura remains obscure. How, for example, does an oil platform in the open sea relate to his projects? Why did Souto de Moura choose this image? Was he fascinated by the contrast between the construction and the immensity of the surrounding ocean? Is he interested in the idea of boring into the ground? Is it about the sublime beauty of infrastructure buildings, or the relation between the fragility of a man-made construction and the enormous yet invisible reservoir of energy it taps into? Another example is the envelope of a pack of Camel cigarettes pinned next to a window. Why would one keep such an item on the wall? Is it because of the cliché of an Arab skyline, the Pyramid, the frame formed by slender columns? Is it

1 Paul Virilio, *Bunker archéologie*, Paris, Centre Georges Pompidou-CCI, 1975.

Miles Davis collage composed for Eduardo Souto de Moura by one of his daughters
Atelier Eduardo Souto de Moura, 2010

the Orientalist iconography that seems to have survived from the nineteenth century, omnipresent yet overlooked on an omnipresent consumer good? Or is this simply the favorite cigarette brand of the architect? And why did he keep the image of the veiled Muslim women taking photographs with their cell phones while their faces are hidden? Did he choose it because of its anachronism, something that he regularly employs in his own buildings, where the old and the new collide? Or does he like it because it depicts the insatiable desire of human beings to take images? Is it about the double voyeurism present in the image—the voyeurism of the photographers, whose faces we cannot see, and our own voyeurism watching them taking pictures that we cannot see? Why does he use airsickness bags from Austrian Airlines for a series of sketches? Is it because they are the very emblems of a kind of vertigo that implicitly features in the work of an architect who tends toward the horizontal, even the underground, whenever possible? Or are they a reference to the Austrian architect Hans Hollein, for instance, to the famous early 1960s' collage of an aircraft carrier in the landscape? And what about the sports images, such as the sumo wrestlers or the soccer player? Can they tell us more about Souto de Moura's fascination for mass, energy, and the elegance of movements? Are these emblems of the way he deals with tectonics, and with gravity in his own work?

What is the function of these images in the architectural practice of Eduardo Souto de Moura? He rarely includes them in documentations or renderings. They are not employed in the sense of OMA, or Herzog & de Meuron, who place some traces from the design process as visual tools in exhibitions and articles, in order to provide a context of interpretation of their built work. In the case of Souto de Moura, the images relate rather to the topics that he touches on in lectures, writings, and interviews. The imagery, I would argue, functions as a reflection of the daily work, as a horizon of the practice. One could characterize it as a kind of visual theory of the oeuvre—and after all, the Greek word *theorein* means "to oversee" or "to look at."

As an ongoing collection, the images in Eduardo Souto de Moura's studio cannot be separated from the architectural practice. In fact, they belong to a long tradition of collections by artists and architects, from John Soane's collection of antique architectural fragments to Ludwig Mies van der Rohe's collection of artworks of the Weimar Republic, to the 1970s' Manhattanism- and Americana-themed postcard collections that Rem Koolhaas and Madelon Vriesendorp kept in two suitcases.[2] The most famous example of such a collection is certainly Gerhard Richter's *Atlas.* It consists of photographs, sketches, and newspaper clippings that Richter has been collecting and arranging on panels since 1962. These historical and personal documents, some of which served as the point of departure for paintings, have grown to be a significant part of the artist's oeuvre; mounted on, by now, more than 700 panels, Richter has been exhibiting them since the early 1970s.[3]

2 See Vivian Endicott Barnett, "The Architect as Art Collector," in Phyllis Lambert (ed.), *Mies in America,* New York, Harry N. Abrams, 2001, pp. 90–131; Shumon Basar, Charlie Koolhaas, "Disasters, Babies, Glass Bricks, Postcard Archaeology," in Shuman Basar, Stephan Trüby (eds.), *The World of Madelon Vriesendorp. Painting, Postcards, Objects, Games,* London, AA Publications, 2008, pp. 74–81.

3 Gerhard Richter, *Atlas,* Cologne, König, 2006; see also www.gerhard-richter.com/art/atlas.

On Atlas's Shoulders

On a more general level, Eduardo Souto de Moura's collection reminds us of earlier attempts to depict the complexity of the present in the guise of an atlas. The most prominent of these image collections in the early twentieth century was Aby Warburg's *Mnemosyne Atlas.* Mounted on boards, Warburg juxtaposed a great variety of images, which helped to locate the tradition of the Antique iconography up to the present day—the so-called *Nachleben,* the Afterlife, of Antiquity. Whereas Warburg mainly operated with images, Walter Benjamin attempted to combine images

Eduardo Souto de Moura, Robinson Foundation, Portalegre, composition with reference images
George Bailey, drawing, 1810

and texts. His *Arcades Project,* left unfinished at the time of his suicide in 1940, and only later published in the form of a book,[4] consists of hundreds of notes, found in newspapers, historic accounts, theories, and in literature. Many are about ordinary life, about advertisement, about habits and mentalities. They belong to the category of sources that historians tended to neglect, but that—like the photographs by Eugène Atget, who depicted the backstage of modern Paris in the phase of its demolition—allow us solely to reconstruct images of the daily life of our forebears. In this monumental project, Benjamin had intended to map the landscape of early capitalism. He focused on the early nineteenth-century Parisian phenomenon of the arcades—collective endeavors that concentrated dozens of small shops in a space that was covered by a glass roof. The disappearance of the arcades in the mid-nineteenth century, their destruction by the urbanization of Baron Haussmann for political, economic, and military reasons, prefigured the process of political and economic monopolization that threatened and eventually destroyed the structure of the Weimar Republic between the wars at the time Benjamin was working. Thus, the *Arcade Project* is also a model of historiography as such. Its fascination is due precisely to its nonlinear structure and its fragmentary state. History, Benjamin tells us, can be represented only in the guise of fragments, or ruins. But there are innumerable links that run between past and present.

Aby Warburg, *Mnemosyne-Atlas*, 1924–29

It is no coincidence that Walter Benjamin's writings, like those of Aby Warburg, were rediscovered in the 1970s and have since then formed part of the collective imagination. For Eduardo Souto de Moura's generation, their oeuvres, and the concept of the atlas in general, was a crucial point of reference. The idea of the atlas became a means of mapping the shifting grounds under their feet. The accumulation and juxtaposition of fragments corresponded to their own scepticism towards the "grand narratives" of modernity, as Jean-François Lyotard put it, and their own experience of the unfulfilled revolution of 1968. The concept of the atlas helps to interrelate phenomena with each other in a situation where everything seems to fall apart. Bernhard and Hilla Becher became famous during this period with their industrial archaeology, their photographic archive of defunct industrial buildings. It is no coincidence that reproductions of their photographic campaigns feature in Souto de Moura's collection. Paul Virilio followed, as mentioned above, the traces of repressed history during the war and outlined the paranoia of his own present time. Aldo Rossi, to name the most influential architect of this phase, made a photographic inventory of the industrial heritage of Northern Italy. In his oeuvre, and in the earthworks that the American artist Robert Smithson produced around 1970, and the architectural performances of Gordon Matta-Clark in the 1970s, the interest in the fragment, the ruin, the concept of entropy, and the museum ran together and paved the ground for the following generation of architects and artists.

Eduardo Souto de Moura's interest in the dimension of history is, in fact, closely related to the legacy of protagonists such as Aldo Rossi, Robert Smithson, and Gordon Matta-Clark. It oscillates between the nostalgic fascination for the ruin and the optimism that the new can draw out of the fragmented past. It allows him to reactivate the historical dimension in architecture, a dimension that is more or less repressed, or compressed, today. Most of today's architectural projects are caught, like all works of visual culture, in the current realm of an eternal present, a state apparently outside history, where the past and the future seem to be condensed in an all-embracing present. The theorists Michael

4 Walter Benjamin, *Paris, capitale du XIXe siècle. Le livre des passages,* ed. Rolf Tiedemann, trans. Jean Lacoste, Paris, Cerf, 1989.

Hardt and Antonio Negri have discussed this phenomenon in their book *Empire,* published in 2000, and their hypothesis that we are entering a phase of the eternal present and that the world is turning into a homogenized, "smooth space" remains highly plausible today.[5]

There are various attempts to resist this homogenization by means of architecture, most commonly, perhaps, the method of the historical quote. Eduardo Souto de Moura's approach is characterized, one could argue, by a method of anachronism, namely the collision of different temporalities. It is not only the "old" and the "new" that intertwine in his oeuvre. It is the problem of dealing with history as such that we can perceive when we look at his buildings. Despite the formal analogies between the Braga Stadium and Antique theaters or amphitheaters mentioned above, this building does not "connect" the present with the past—say, the idea of today's mass-mediated sports industry with the political and social role of the theater and circus in ancient Greece, or Rome. Rather, it focuses on the breaches between the contemporary and the past and thus makes clear that the present is entirely disconnected from the past, that there is no such thing as historical coherence, no linearity, only chaos. Souto de Moura's predilection for the Cyclopean wall, which is evident in his collection of images and many of his projects, namely, walls made out of large stones or boulders, is symptomatic of this approach. In the Cyclopean wall, the elements are juxtaposed without mortar,

Atelier Eduardo Souto de Moura, archive, 2010

held together by gravity and friction. No single stone resembles the other; there is no such thing as homogeneity. Unlike the method of collage, or montage, where the individual elements are placed in front of a common ground, this juxtaposition does not hide difference but emphasizes the rawness and internal contradiction of the building process itself.

The images in Eduardo Souto de Moura's collection are thus never passive items of a collection but active agents in an ongoing process. Their function recalls the earlier concept of the image as something that is never static but constantly in motion. At the turn of the nineteenth to the twentieth century, the French philosopher Henri Bergson, in his book *Matter and Memory,* had already defined the image as "a certain existence that is more than that which the idealist calls a representation but less than that which the realist calls a *thing*—an existence placed halfway between the 'thing' and the 'representation.'"[6] And for Jean-Paul Sartre, the image exists as "an act as much as a thing."[7] This might explain the fact that Souto de Moura does not want to fix the order of his images. In keeping them afloat he can constantly rearrange them without fixing their meaning. They maintain their potential as mobile elements in an ongoing play. They form a virtually endless repertoire of playing cards, which can be reshuffled over and over again and partake in a genuinely experimental architecture, a process more interested in questions than answers.

5 Michael Hardt, Antonio Negri, *Empire,* Cambridge, Harvard University Press, 2000, p. XIII.

6 Henri Bergson, *Matter and Memory,* trans. Nancy Margaret Paul and W. Scott Palmer, George Allen and Unwin, 1911, pp. XI–XII.

7 As cited in Hans Belting, *Bild-Anthropologie, Entwürfe für eine Bildwissenschaft,* Munich, Wilhelm Fink, 2001, p. 7.

Atelier Eduardo Souto de Moura, archive, 2010

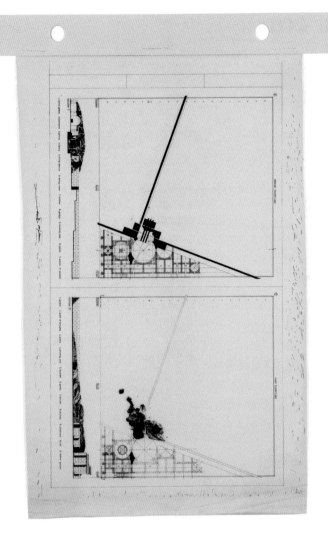

Eduardo Souto de Moura, a house for Karl Friedrich Schinkel, 1979

Amarcord:
Analogy and Architecture

Diogo Seixas Lopes

Ever the pragmatist, Eduardo Souto de Moura makes clear how analogy works for him. It is the process that converts images, drawn from memory and personal belongings, into architecture. Visual and literary references construct a "mental Neufert,"[1] sparking correspondences during design. Like a secret weapon, this operation reconciles professional obligations with biographic indulgences. "The only biography is of an unproductive life," wrote Roland Barthes.[2] In order to solve this contradiction, recollections are used as a repertoire for projects. Analogy allows for the transfer since "no sooner is a form seen than it must resemble something: humanity seems doomed to Analogy and, finally, to Nature."[3] Thus, Eduardo Souto de Moura is able to merge the public and private spheres of his life. Throughout, analogy has always been a muse. This text examines its presence along the timeline of the architect.

Analogy can be defined as the similarity between things otherwise unlike, bound by a sense of proportion. This meaning derives

1 Eduardo Souto de Moura, "Biographic Interview," in Antonio Esposito, Giovanni Leoni, *Eduardo Souto de Moura,* Milan, Electa, 2003, p. 438 [interview by Monica Daniele].

2 Roland Barthes, *Roland Barthes par Roland Barthes,* Paris, Seuil, 1975, p. 6. "Car tel est le sens théorique de cette limitation: manifester que le temps du récit (de l'imagerie) finit avec la jeunesse du sujet: il n'y a de biographie que de la vie improductive."

3 *Ibid.,* p. 48.

Le Corbusier, *Vers une architecture,* 1923

from the Greek origin of the word, *analogia,* evolving into the relation of features increasingly complex and abstract. As noted, "*it emerged as a form of dialectics attempting to bridge the seen and the unseen, the known and the unknown.*"[4] A case in point: Saint Thomas Aquinas was able to equate the attributes of God to those of earthly creatures. These parallels seek to explain the phenomena of the world according to a ratio that connects them. In other words, A is to B what C is to D. Images are at the heart of this mode of cognition. They make visible ideas hard to grasp, giving rise to insight. Hence, their combination becomes an alchemic quest for knowledge. An atlas, like the one presented in this book, collects and sorts them with the same purpose. It is an intellectual laboratory in which new materials are fabricated.

When applied to architecture, analogy enables the transposition of disparate facts. Scale, location, and time can be exchanged with each other in order to outline a particular reasoning. A notable example of this possibility is the equivalence established by Leon Battista Alberti regarding the city and the house: "If (as the philosophers maintain) the city is like some large house, and the house is in turn like some small city, cannot the various parts of the house—atria, *xysti,* dining rooms, porticoes, and so on—be considered miniature buildings?"[5] The analogy served to convey general rules of design but also a bond between "domus" and "polis," fundamental to humanism. Centuries later, another famed comparison also encapsulated an epoch. In *Vers une architecture,*

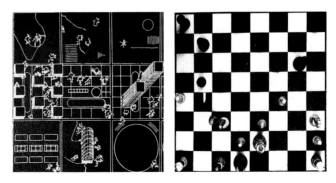

Oswald Mathias Ungers, *Morphologie. City Metaphors,* 1982

Le Corbusier juxtaposed Greek temples—Paestum (600 BC), Parthenon (447 BC)—with automobiles—Humbert (1907), Delage Grand-Sport (1921)—to illustrate the notion of standard.[6] This quartet composed a visual rhetoric, typical of Modernism, embracing a discourse of progress, culture, and technology subsumed to the credo of the "state of the art." Again, analogy was instrumental to depict this thought.[7]

Today, it is no longer possible to be so assured about ideas and images. Despite systematic attempts to classify them, their dissemination provokes inevitable ambivalence. Nevertheless, analogical association looks for significance among particular instances. Therefore, it is still a way to find a form for solutions. When problems concern architecture, this implies a course of action in the expanded field of the discipline. As Oswald Mathias Ungers argued:

"If, for instance, designing is understood purely technically, then it results in pragmatic functionalism or in mathematical formulas. If designing is exclusively an expression of psychological experiences, then only emotional values matter, and it turns into a religious substitute. If, however, the physical reality is understood and conceptualized as an analogy to our imagination of that reality, then we pursue a morphological design concept, turning into phenomena that, like all real concepts, can be expanded or condensed; they can be seen as polarities contradicting or complementing each other, existing as pure concepts in themselves like a piece of art."[8]

These explanations introduce a series of "city metaphors" listed by the German architect. Pairs of urban plans and photographs, each with a caption, express certain concepts. Similarity: Ivan Leonidov's Magnitogorsk (1930) next to a chessboard. Stretching: Lucio Costa's Brasilia (1957) next to an airplane. And so forth. But some of the couplings produce surprising effects, such as the scheme for an ideal town in Kentucky side by side with the picture of wooden crates amid a snowy field. Inside one of the crates is an abandoned baby. This disturbing image defies any rationale on the link to its referent. It echoes a description given by Carl Gustav Jung in a letter addressed to Sigmund Freud: "Logical

4 Barbara Maria Stafford, *Visual Analogy: Consciousness as the Art of Connecting,* Cambridge, MA, MIT Press, 1999, p. 8. For a historical overview of analogy see James F. Ross, *Portraying Analogy,* Cambridge, Cambridge University Press, 1981.

5 Leon Battista Alberti, *De Re Aedificatoria* (circa 1486)/*On the Art of Building in Ten Books,* trans. Joseph Rykwert, Neil Leach, and Robert Tavernor, Cambridge, MA, MIT Press, 1988, p. 23.

6 Le Corbusier, *Vers une architecture,* Paris, Crés, 1923, pp. 106–07.

7 For an extensive analysis of this and other architectural analogies see Jean-Pierre Chupin, *Analogie et théorie en architecture. De la vie, de la ville et de la conception, même,* Gollion, Infolio, 2010.

8 Oswald Mathias Ungers, *Morphologie. City Metaphors,* Cologne, Walther König, 1982, pp. 8–9.

thinking is 'verbal thinking.' Analogical thinking is archaic, unconscious, not put into words, and hardly formulable in words."[9]

Eduardo Souto de Moura has been aware of the disquieting nature of analogy since the start of his métier. The sketches that precede this text are proof. Reminiscent of the postmodernist exploits of Michael Graves or Charles Moore, these studies show assemblages of columns and pediments. Some of them produce a virtual double, reflected in water. A side note deems unfit the inverted image of classicism, while there is also a reference to "fascism as a cover-up." But the drawings evidence mannerism and irony, like a "guilty pleasure." They are the antithesis of a project from the same period, the housing for São Vitor in Porto (1974–79). Eduardo Souto de Moura participated in the design, supervised by Álvaro Siza under the auspices of SAAL. At the time, he viewed the political engagement of this operation as a "promised land."[10] But there was also the desire for "architecture dans le boudoir." The historicist follies in the sketches evoke the expression coined by Manfredo Tafuri, and his verdict:

"Today, he who is willing to make architecture speak is forced to rely on materials empty of any and all meaning: he is forced to reduce to degree zero all architectonic ideology, all dreams of social function, and any utopian residues. In his hands, the elements of the modern architectural tradition come suddenly to be reduced to enigmatic fragments, to mute signals of a language whose code has been lost, stuffed away casually in the desert of history."[11]

Remembrance of the past casts a long shadow, indelible from the present. Scattered like debris, heritage distorts any linear narrative of events. Since these naïve beliefs expired, it has been necessary to venture into the labyrinths of memory and search for a way out. Therefore, architecture is destined to be *ars combinatoria*. Analogy is a tool, finding threads between different sources. Such is the case of the House for Karl Friedrich Schinkel (1979), an entry for a competition organized in Japan under the judging of James Stirling. His assignment challenged the imagination:

"In the hypothetical situation posited for this competition, after achieving success, Schinkel asks his very brilliant pupil (you, the contestant) to design a family house for him. This pupil is indeed gifted because he has foreseen in his daydreams the entire development of the modern movement up to 1980. Therefore, he (you) can assume that the competition requires a modern or neoclassical house, or a modern neoclassical or classic neo-modern, or any mixture he likes."[12]

Eduardo Souto de Moura responded to this eclectic freedom with absolute control. His proposal was an abstract composition using archetypal figures such as the ruin, the grotto, and the villa as readymades. Within the boundaries of the house, there was also a stream, orchards, woodlands, and a hill. Fully enclosed by walls of stone, these grounds formed a *hortus conclusus*. Placed near the oil refinery of Matosinhos, it used this industrial archaeology as an imprint for the residence. The proximity to the Boa Nova Tea House and Leça Swimming Pools by Álvaro Siza underlined pedigree rather than style. All these allusions were intentionally orchestrated throughout the project, as a layer of double meanings. An early trial for subsequent works, this sophisticated collage of ideas celebrated the quintessential nature of architecture. That is, *cosa mentale*.

Direct reference for analogy as a design method lies in the work and the writings of Aldo Rossi. He anticipated the autonomy of this procedure in a seminal essay, discussing his craft as "architecture for museums."[13] It was heralded with an emblematic painting

9 Carl Gustav Jung to Sigmund Freud, March 2, 1910, in *The Freud/Jung Letters,* ed. William McGuire, trans. Ralph Manheim and R.F.C. Hull, London, Hogarth, 1974, pp. 298–99.

10 Eduardo Souto de Moura, October 1980, Apprenticeship Report, Archive Eduardo Souto de Moura, Porto, p. 8.

11 Manfredo Tafuri, "L'Architecture dans le boudoir: The language of criticism and the criticism of language," trans. Victor Caliandro, *Oppositions,* no. 3 (May 1974), p. 38.

12 James Stirling, "A House for Karl Friedrich Schinkel," *Japan Architect,* no. 274, February 1980, p. 9.

13 Aldo Rossi, "Architettura per i musei," in Guido Canella et al., *Teoria della progettazione architettonica,* Bari, Dedalo, 1968, pp. 123–37.

Álvaro Siza, SAAL housing program, São Vitor, Porto, 1974–77

by Canaletto, depicting Venice. In *Capriccio palladiano* (1755–59), several projects by Andrea Palladio compose a *veduta*. While none of them actually exists in the city, they nevertheless convey its identity. "Such objects are situated between inventory and memory. Regarding the question of memory, architecture is also transformed into autobiographical experience: places and things change with the superimposition of a new meanings."[14] Using recollections to transfigure the real, Eduardo Souto de Moura pursued the same course. Under the avowed influence of his Italian mentor, he settled his lineage: "To be Rossian means to me understanding culture, understanding the history of one's own city, of one's own places, of one's own memory, and intertwining them, following a personal and emotional logic."[15]

Perhaps heterodoxy is the condition of being Portuguese. Faced with perennial difficulties and the mirage of historical deeds, it is necessary to adjust to great contrasts. Against the odds, some were able to strive for the universal amid such a singular environment. Eduardo Lourenço emphasized the importance of this trait since "in knowledge or action, philosophy or politics, man is a divided reality. Heterodoxy is the respect for this division."[16] Throughout an entire career, Eduardo Souto de Moura has consistently reclaimed the right to diversity. Naturally, historiography praised the canonical aspects of discipline and continuity. These values spring from the professional reality and are handled with common sense. But there are other ambitions that defy protocol, despite the risk of misunderstandings. "Yet it is still vital for each and every one of us to take a personal chance into an almost predictable failure."[17]

It is possible to trace profound changes in the work of Eduardo Souto de Moura by the nature of the analogies employed. Initial projects often resorted to citations within the disciplinary field, appointing a primordial pantheon of elective affinities. Among them, there rose the figure of Mies van der Rohe as the definitive embodiment of the modern architect. This fascination, if not obsession, made a mark on projects such as the SEC Cultural Centre in Porto (1981–91) and the house in Alcanena (1987–92). Other references also flourished, from Villa Adriana to Guiseppe Terragni, but the legacy of the German master prevailed. His insignia of transparency and freestanding plans was interlaced with vernacular tectonics for the buildings, precise and tactile at once. The extensive use of stone masonry and manipulation of ruins did not surrender to the picturesque. Rather, it made tangible the presence of time as a "great destroyer." Architecture is a means to seize this motion, against the grain of the everyday. While bound to failure, it must push forward and leave something behind.

The recurrent mentions of Eduardo Souto de Moura with regard to a performance by Joseph Beuys, *Coyote: I Like America and America Likes Me* (1974), are made under the same premise: "I am interested in the action that transpires in Beuys's experiment, its result and not its locale. It's all the same if the gallery was tall or long, if it was in New York or in São Pedro de Rio Seco; the important thing was 'time,' the permanence in 'place,' and the selection of the materials."[18] The sway of contemporary art allowed for other possibilities and analogies. They became object-based, drawing from the humor of Marcel Duchamp and the rigor of Donald Judd. Thus, the Burgo Tower in Porto (1991–2007) resembled a pile of stacked crates, and the cantilever of one of the Two Houses in Ponte de Lima (2001–02) was compared to a bottle holder. It is unclear if these visual puns precede or succeed the projects. One way or the other, they downplay the cultured in

14 Aldo Rossi, "An Analogical Architecture," trans. David Stewart, *A+U: Architecture and Urbanism*, no. 65, May 1976, p. 74. The projects by Palladio are the Rialto Bridge, the Chiericati Palace, and the Palladian Basilica. The first is a study, while the others are in Vicenza.

15 Eduardo Souto de Moura, "Su Aldo Rossi," in "Dopo Aldo Rossi," *d'Architettura*, no. 23, April 2004, p. 189.

16 Eduardo Lourenço, *Heterodoxia I*, Coimbra, Coimbra, 1949, p. 15.

17 *Ibid.*, p. 27.

18 Eduardo Souto de Moura, "Time," in "Eduardo Souto de Moura. Recent Work," *2G*, no. 5, 2008, p. 138. São Pedro de Rio Seco is the birthplace of the philosopher Eduardo Lourenço.

Canaletto, *Capriccio palladiano,* 1755–59
Eduardo Souto de Moura, house in Alcanena, 1987–92

favor of the prosaic. While it is highbrow to use the notion of "as found," architecture merely aspires to be yet another thing.

Over the last years, this work has struggled against its own stasis. The condition was crystallized in the stereotypical solution of the glass box, replicated as a trademark. In science, the glass box is the symbol for an intelligible process whereas the black box stands for a more opaque backstage of knowledge. Deflecting Pavlovian repetition from disciples and copycats, Eduardo Souto de Moura delved into the latter. His analogical thinking is now closer to the definition of Carl Gustav Jung, archaic and unconscious. Many projects display a subversive glee, shaping familiar images into unfamiliar buildings. The protruding boxes of the Cinema House in Porto (1999–2000) bring to mind the beady eyes of a gigantic fly that landed in the heart of the city. Likewise, the six houses for Villa Utopia Resort (2006) progress from the profile of an anteater into a more abstract configuration. This transition oscillates between a zoomorphic extravaganza by Jean-Jacques Lequeu and the typological formulas of Jean-Nicolas-Louis Durand. In other words, A is to B what C is to D.

Eduardo Souto de Moura has been hailed for his no-nonsense approach towards the hardships of clients, contracts, and construction sites. They are skillfully tackled in order to get things done. But the pragmatic spirit of the architect also resides in the ability to protect intimacy under a social persona. He is thus able to mastermind the coexistence of public virtues and private vices.

Joseph Beuys, *Coyote: I Like America and America Likes Me,* 1974

The duality inevitably recalls the characters of Dr. Jekyll and Mr. Hyde. A snapshot of this "double exposure" was the installation *Object Light* in Porto (1996). An acrylic screen, transparent and blue, divided the exhibition space in two. At the back of this cell, there was a black panel with a grid of blue lamps. Up front, an amplifier and computer converted into light the sounds of Miles Davis and his classic *Kind of Blue* (1959). With a swarm of soft flashes, the acrylic screen veiled the rigid apparatus of the lighting fixtures. Exposed and concealed, these layers could be a portrait of Eduardo Souto de Moura and his inclinations. They range from music to architecture, from Miles to Mies.

The atlas presented in this book is a collection of *objets trouvés,* randomly sorted throughout the years. It comprises photographs, postcards, clippings, memorabilia, and other findings. This jumble of things reveals an insatiable appetite for the many faces of reality. Nevertheless, it is possible to find an order in such chaos. Each project offers the chance to ransom certain items, for the sake of inspiration. The kaleidoscopic nature of this supply denotes compulsion, but also restraint. As Aldo Rossi observed:

"Yet there is a path to salvation in such acts of classification; the catalog rediscovers a secret and unexpected history of the image; its very artificiality becomes fantasy. Once everything has stopped forever, there is something to see: the little backgrounds of the yellowish photos, the unexpected appearance of an

 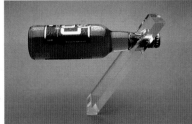

Eduardo Souto de Moura, two houses in Ponte de Lima, 2001–02, and bottle support as reference image

19 Aldo Rossi, *A Scientific Autobiography*, Cambridge, MA, MIT Press, 1981, p. 47.

20 Eduardo Souto de Moura, 2008, Competition for the Multifunctional Building of the Serralves Foundation in Matosinhos, Archive Eduardo Souto de Moura. "O lago, as ruínas e a chaminé são já por si um 'Chirico,' que fomos descobrindo e não quisemos rejeitar."

interior, the very dust on an image in which one recognizes the value of time."[19]

Eduardo Souto de Moura continues to explore his archive, searching for new trophies. This design method can be likened to the technique of *cadavre exquis,* juxtaposing miscellaneous sources. Among recent samples, it is worthwhile to probe into the competition entry for the Multifunctional Building of the Serralves Foundation in Matosinhos (2008). Planned as a facility to store and display contemporary art, the project was an anthology. It started with the zigzag silhouette of sheds, linked to a block epitomizing the style of the architect: "Souto de Moura d'aprés Souto de Moura." Then, a steel tower crammed together the machinery in a disconcerting combination of the image of a robot with those of Bernhard and Hilla Becher. The facility enclosed an existing pond within a courtyard, crowned by a tall chimney of brick from the disused factory on the site. While part of an industrial archaeology, this vertical element was also a tribute: "The lake, the ruins, and the factory are themselves a 'Chirico' we discovered and did not want to reject."[20] The scheme had a striking resemblance to *Metaphysical Interior with Large Factory* (1916–17), one of the famous paintings by Giorgio de Chirico. Like surreal props, they were pasted in the renderings of the proposal. These photomontages were remakes of *pittura metafisica,* updated.

Iconography pervaded other works, notably the Paula Rego Museum in Cascais (2005–09), as if the buildings were "calli-

Eduardo Souto de Moura, *Objecto Luz* exhibition, Porto, 1996

grams." They are the emblem of an idea, confiscated from images and texts. "In its millennial tradition, the calligram has a triple role: to augment the alphabet, to repeat something without the aid of rhetoric, to trap things in a double cipher."[21] The explanation, by Michel Foucault, applies to this architecture. Analogy encodes it with the language of autobiography, signed by Eduardo Souto de Moura. The universal status it seeks is therefore related to this kind of personification. "The space occupied by analogies is really a space of radiation. Man is surrounded by it on every side; but, inversely, he transmits these resemblances back into the world from which he receives them."[22]

In a sketch named *Magritte,* two disproportionate apples crowd the atrium of the laboratory and office building for Novartis in Basel (2005–11). Amid the headquarters of a pharmaceutical company, this fantasy implies a subtitle: *ceci n'est pas un building.* It counters with nonchalance the respect for regulations that seems to confirm a "tendency to obey the constraints with an almost masochistic pleasure."[23] Eduardo Souto de Moura treasures these contradictions, the true sign of an author. Despite biographical indulgences, he is well aware of professional obligations: "There is a sort of automatic writing, like in music or literature. But we cannot bury our mistakes. They petrify forever."[24] Yet the atlas remains his book of disquiet. In a time when most things expire quickly, he holds on to this valuable property. *Amarcord.*

21 Michel Foucault, *Ceci n'est pas une pipe,* Montpellier, Fata Morgana, 1973 / *This Is Not a Pipe,* trans. and ed. James Harkness, Berkeley, CA, University of California Press, 2008, p. 20.

22 Michel Foucault, *Les mots et les choses. Une archéologie des sciences humaines,* Paris, Gallimard, 1966 / *The Order of Things: An Archaeology of the Human Sciences,* Oxon, Routledge, 2002, p. 26.

23 Ákos Moravánszky, "The City of the Captive South. Álvaro Siza, Peter Märkli and Eduardo Souto de Moura on the Novartis Campus," in Delfim Sardo (ed.), *Let's Talk About Houses. Between North and South,* Lisbon, Athena, 2010, p. 256.

24 Eduardo Souto de Moura, "Os traços em volta," interview by Maria Leonor Nunes, *Jornal de Letras,* April 6–19, 2011.

Giorgio de Chirico, *Interno metafisico con grande officina,* 1916

Eduardo Souto de Moura, *Novartis laboratories*, Basel, 2005–11

Atelier Eduardo Souto de Moura, 2012

A Rather Unscientific Autobiography

Eduardo Souto de Moura

I was born in Porto, Portugal, in 1952. In 1958, I started attending the Italian school about 100 meters from my home. For four years I had teachers whom I recall with affection, such as Ms. Morelli and the music teacher, Mr. Facciola, who introduced me to Roman culture and the Italian language, resulting in an early admiration for classicism that has never left me.

The five years of secondary school were a sort of Middle Ages, a *nuit obscure,* where learning French was compulsory, opening the door to the existentialism then in fashion: Sartre, Camus, Boris Vian, etc, but above all, Rimbaud. "Il faut être absolument moderne." It was with that conviction that I entered the School of Fine Arts in the 1970s to study architecture.

The first years focused on the social sciences, "Marxism," sociology, anthropology, structuralism, etc. The professors believed that project synthesis could occur by dominating the analytical disciplines. Our class manual was Saussure's linguistic course. Drawing, in a time of revolution, was something technocratic and reactionary.

During the "Carnation Revolution," the state secretary for housing, who was an architect (Nuno Portas), founded the Mobile Service for Local Support (SAAL), which economically backed student brigades so that they could conceive projects for residents' associations. Common sense was our luck. Since we had no idea how to plan things, we asked a professional with experience in the area. Álvaro Siza accepted and I worked in his studio for five years. I learned from his character how to resolve problems, to build the project, slowly learning about reality and its history. The definitive solutions I never used, out of a sense of embarrassment.

I already knew about Aldo Rossi's famous article "Architettura per i musei" when he was my professor in Santiago de Compostela. At that project seminar, we finally understood the discipline's autonomy, which was questioned in the classes we found hard to attend because of our work with Siza: São Vítor, Évora, Bouça, Berlim, etc. For reasons that I understood later, Álvaro Siza let me go as a collaborator, maintaining (definitively) that it was not the ideal process for making me an architect.

Next, I worked with my urbanism professor, Fernandes de Sá, who gave me the Braga market project, which I built. Jean Nouvel chose it for the Paris Biennial in the 1980s. After two years of military service, I was able to win a competition for a cultural center in Porto, which I was also able to build. I had organized the basis for getting started on my independent professional practice and was ready to help rebuild a country after forty-eight years of dictatorship. To give an idea: half a million houses had to be built.

Portugal obviously worked differently from Europe. Venturi and Aldo Rossi had proposed postmodernism. But Lyotard didn't convince me because Salazarism had been a sort of postmodernism, which was strange because we were "post" without ever having been "modern." I was closer to Habermas and his criticism of the Venice Biennial and approached Mies van der Rohe for the opportunity offered by his principles at that time of change. Before cardboard fronts, *less is more* was truly a breath of fresh air. Like modern movement, neoplasticism, industrial construction as future and permanence of the classic but with modern materials.

As a professor in Switzerland, in Lausanne and Zurich, and later at Harvard, I became friends with Jacques Herzog. He was clear-sighted enough during the impasse of the 1980s to work with local culture, the vernacular language, and contemporary art. His work showed that "the universal is local, without walls" (Miguel Torga). In Zurich, I also got to know Donald Judd, who marked me with his explanation of sculpture and drawing, of wanting to be an architect.

Now, thirty years later, I continue working with Siza, and with pleasure. I see Herzog regularly and collect books and images of Mies. One of the most recent I found showed Mies at home with the windows closed, reclining in a silk robe on an ordinary velvet settee, not a fashionable design, and drinking a martini. On another postcard, I found the master sitting on an anonymous sofa, reading under a lampshade and surrounded by Klee and Kandinsky paintings, Picasso sculptures, records, most likely Bach, and books surely by St. Augustine. Mies always cited St. Augustine, saying that "beauty mirrors truth," but Mies lied. He constantly lied in the construction details, which were always covered with more showy materials. It is this contradiction that interests me more in his work. Mies had an all-glass apartment on Lake Shore Drive, but he never moved there. He always lived within walls, in the shade, surrounded by artworks. To find out why Mies never moved house is to understand what will become of architecture.

Acceptance speech delivered in June 2010 in Paris upon receiving a medal from the Académie d'Architecture de France,

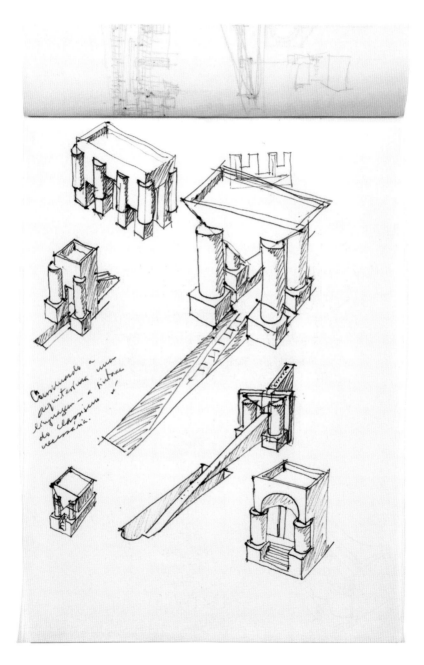

Eduardo Souto de Moura, sketches, 1970s

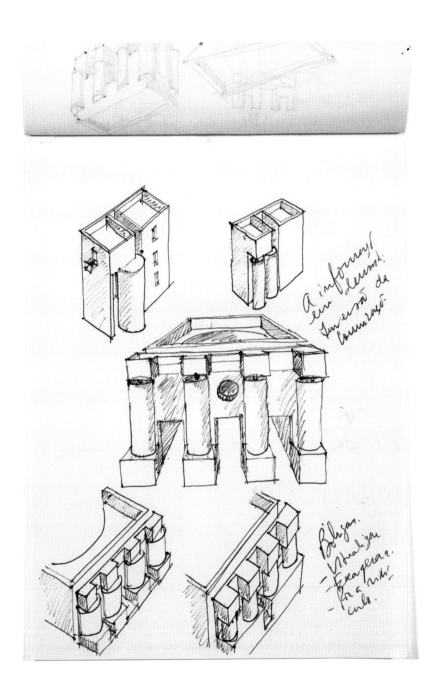

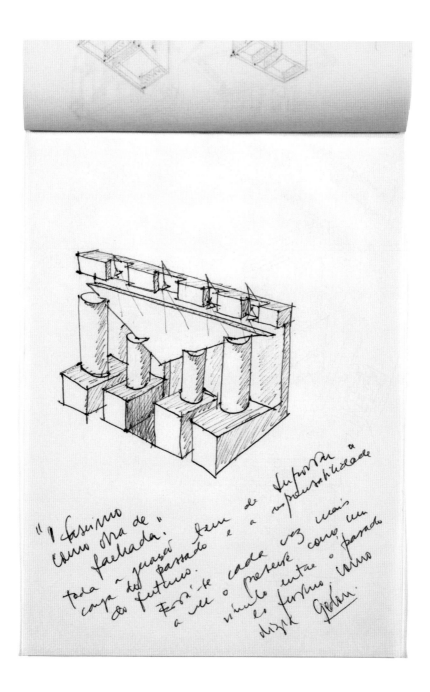

"O fascínio como obra de fachada."

toda a proposta tem de supor-se a impossibilidade
como do passado e a impossibilidade
do futuro.

Será-se cada vez mais
a ver o presente como um
vínculo entre o passado
disse Gideu.

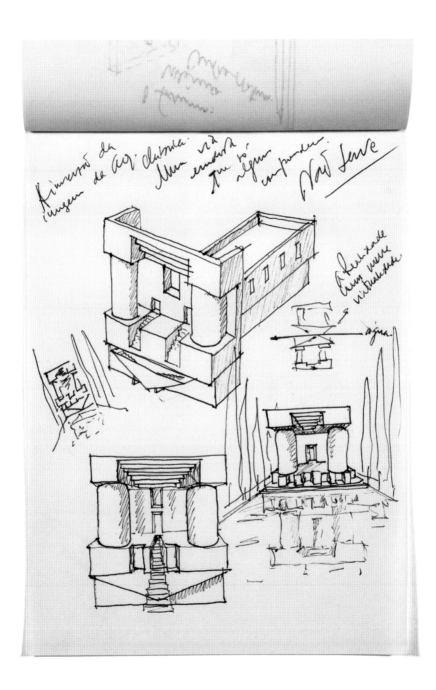

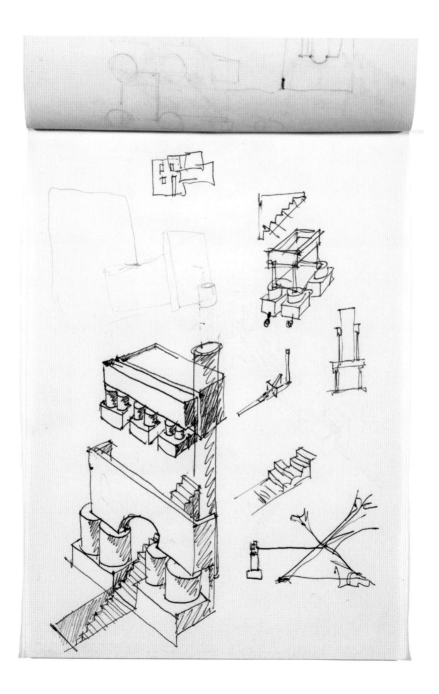

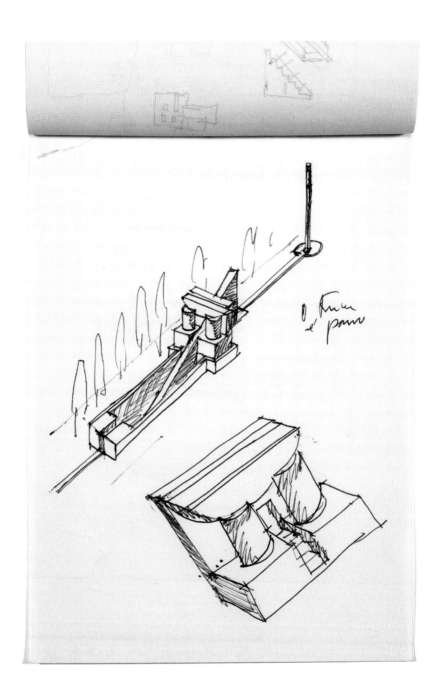

la tua
el pane

FLOATING IMAGES
EDUARDO SOUTO DE MOURA'S WALL ATLAS

Edited by André Tavares and Pedro Bandeira

Translations: John Bradford (texts by
Pedro Bandeira and Eduardo Souto de Moura)
Coordination: Sophie Loschert
Copyediting: Danko Szabó
Design: Integral Lars Müller/Sarah Pia and Lars Müller
Prepress: Ast & Fischer, Wabern, Switzerland
Printing and binding: Kösel, Altusried-Krugzell, Germany
Paper: Hello Fat Matt, 150 g/m²

Original edition: *Eduardo Souto de Moura.*
Atlas de Parede. Imagens de Método
© 2011 Dafne Editora and Eduardo Souto de Moura

Lars Müller Publishers
Zürich, Switzerland
www.lars-mueller-publishers.com

ISBN 978-3-03778-301-6

Printed in Germany